T0196458

JESUS AND NON-CHRISTIAN RELIGIONS

Interreligious Dialogue After Vatican II And The
Universal Significance Of Jesus

FR. KIERAN C. OKORO, PH.D.

authorHOUSE®

AuthorHouse™
1663 Liberty Drive
Bloomington, IN 47403
www.authorhouse.com
Phone: 1-800-839-8640

Published by AuthorHouse   05/21/2012

ISBN: 978-1-4685-9794-3 (sc)
ISBN: 978-1-4685-9795-0 (e)

Any people depicted in stock imagery provided by Thinkstock are models, and such images are being used for illustrative purposes only.
Certain stock imagery © Thinkstock.

This book is printed on acid-free paper.

CONTENTS

INTRODUCTION

"Outside the Church there is no salvation," is a statement that is usually charged with or evokes a lot of emotion. Since it was first made in the early history of the Church it usually finds itself embroiled in controversy. The controversies are not always only between Christians and non-Christians or only between Catholics and non-Catholics but also sometimes even between Catholics and Catholics. Thus in the late 1940s that statement triggered off a bitter disagreement between Father Leonard Feeney and his St. Benedict Center on the one hand and the archdiocese of Boston under Archbishop Gushing on the other. It is interesting to note that this time the official Church as represented by this archdiocese was on the side opposing the statement while Father Feeney and his followers insisted on it. At the end, when the case was taken to Rome, the Vatican backed the archdiocese of Boston and Father Feeney lost the debate.

On September 5, 2000 the Congregation for the Doctrine of the Faith issued a document, *Dominus Jesus,* clarifying the Church's teaching on the salvific universality of Jesus and the uniqueness of the Church as a way of salvation. Scarcely was this document issued when many, including some Catholics, began to see it as merely restating the age-old "Outside the Church there is no salvation." Those who saw the document that way expressed their dismay; some were ready to begin a controversy. There was no need for that, however. The problem here was and still is a little misunderstanding of the Church's stand with regard to non-Christian religions.

The Church surely does not say that salvation is for only Christians or Catholics only for Jesus won salvation for all. It rather sees all human beings as made by God who loves everyone and wishes all to be saved. It teaches that all men have a common origin and one destiny, namely, God. This is the over-riding reason

1

the Church since the Second Vatican Council has led the way in the promotion of dialogue with not only other Christians but also non-Christian religions.

There is another reason. The Church is quite aware that thanks to human advancement, especially in the areas of communication and transportation, our world is continually becoming smaller and smaller. It has become as it were a global village. On the eve of December 31, 1999, for instance, those living in Los Angeles area were able to watch over their television sets the jubilation of almost every country in the world in the celebrations ushering in the year 2000. It is now possible for a man to finish his business transactions in Tokyo on Saturday morning and attend religious service or Mass in Rome the following day. It is possible for him to be in his office in New York and over the internet transact business in Hong Kong or Bombay. Furthermore, owing largely to the same reason, people of different religious faiths today sometimes work in the same office or company; often they live in the same nation or the same neighborhood or even in the same building. Lack of good relationship or rather religious harmony between them inevitably leads to tensions and often to violent confrontations. The Church wants to obviate these through inter-religious dialogue.

The Church has done a lot of work to promote inter-religious dialogue since the Second Vatican Council. It has also since the same period issued a lot of documents regarding both dialogue and salvation of non-Christians by Jesus. It is very difficult to understand from one document alone the true position of the Church on these matters. This book offers help to overcome that difficulty. It summarizes the Church's teaching on salvation in non-Christian religions and also on inter-religious dialogue from the Second Vatican Council to the present and endeavors to show the universal salvific significance of Jesus.

My special thanks go to Cardinal Francis Arinze, former president of the Pontifical Council for Inter-religious Dialogue who provided useful information, especially for chapter one. I am indebted too to my friends Fr. Gregory Okorobia, Ph. D., Dr. Aldo and Mrs. Mary Anne Trovato, Dr. David and Mrs. Anne Walsh for their encouragement. My gratitude also goes to Tom Craven whose technical support facilitated the editing of this edition.

CHAPTER ONE

INTER-RELIGIOUS DIALOGUE: ITS MEANING AND REASONS FOR IT TODAY

General View

Before we discuss Jesus and non-Christian religions it is quite essential that we know the efforts the Catholic Church has made to bring about friendly relations between it and these religions and the positive statements it has made about them.

Thus the current position of the Catholic Church on non-Christian religions is moderate. It steers a middle course between two extreme positions: on the one hand that of conservative Evangelicals who deny the possibility of salvation in non-Christian religions and on the other that of liberal theologians who see no difference between these religions and the Church as a way of salvation. In its declaration on the Church's relationship to non-Christians, *Nostra Aetate,* the Second Vatican Council states that all human beings "share the same destiny, namely God. His providence, evident goodness, and saving designs extend to all men."[1] It observes that men look to their different religions for solutions to universal existential problems. Such problems include: the meaning of man, the meaning and purpose of life, the content of human behavior which makes this behavior upright or otherwise sinful, the origin and purpose of suffering. Others include: the means to genuine happiness, the meaning of death and what follows after death, and "finally what is the ultimate mystery, beyond human explanation which embraces our entire existence, from which we take our origin and toward which we tend?"[2]

In his capacity as secretary of the Vatican Secretariat for Non-Christian Religions (now Secretariat for Inter-religious Dialogue), Monsignor Pietro Rossano comments on this conciliar statement and other documents. He observes that, "these universal questions are rooted in the very structure of humankind, and therefore reveal a specific dimension of the human person", that is, the innate insatiable hunger or quest for the spiritual, for happiness, that is in all human beings.[3]

All men of all beliefs are involved in this search or quest for happiness; it reveals man's quest for his ultimate cause and ultimate end. Rossano points out that the varying natures of this quest or the corresponding variety of replies to the longing, the ethnic characters, the ecological, historical and cultural experiences of the people as well as the charisma of the religious founders are among the forces that combine to give birth to religious pluralism.[4]

Hence the Catholic Church today "rejects nothing of what is true and holy" in non-Christian religions. Rather it has high "regard for the manner of life and conduct, the precepts and the doctrines" which in various ways differ from her teaching and yet "often reflect a ray of that truth which enlightens all men."[5] And lying hidden among them are the "seeds of the Word" and other "riches which a generous God has distributed among the nations."[6] Because of these positive values, the Church directs Christians to "enter with prudence and charity into discussion and collaboration" with adherents of these religions. And while they have to witness to their own faith and way of life, they should also "acknowledge, preserve and encourage the spiritual and moral truths found" among non-Christians religions, in their social life and culture.[7] The Church sees these religions as different ways of searching for happiness, man's highest good or God. Pope John Paul II puts it succinctly thus: "Though the routes taken may he different, there is but a single goal to which is directed the deepest aspiration of the human spirit as expressed in its quest for God."[8] Yet, the Church makes it clear that "the redeemer of man, Jesus Christ . . . , the center of the universe and of history,"[9] "the key to decipher all the religious traditions of humankind,"[10] is not one of these routes or ways. He is regarded rather as the way and the truth which these other religions are searching for often without knowing it. Thus today the Catholic Church sees some positive qualities in non-Christian religions and seeks dialogue with them. In this chapter we shall consider briefly the meaning of inter-religious dialogue in general as the Church sees it. We shall also consider the reasons why the Catholic Church adopts its positive attitude today toward non-Christian religions.

Meaning of Inter-religious Dialogue

Dialogue is the name that the Church generally gives to its positive attitude toward non-Christian religions or its relationship with them. According to Cardinal Francis Arinze, former president of the Vatican Secretariat for Inter-religious Dialogue, inter-religious dialogue is not simply peaceful coexistence or mutual tolerance. Nor is it a merely academic study of religions; it is not simply exchange of information about different religions. While it is not opposed to conversion, inter-religious dialogue in its general nature is not exactly the same thing as proclamation of the gospel message. And it cannot be identified as an effort toward a syncretistic union of several religions. Inter-religious dialogue is rather

> a meeting of heart and mind . . . a communication between two [or more] believers [of different religious faiths] at the religious level . . . walking together towards truth and working together in projects of common concern . . . . It is a religious partnership without complexes and without hidden agenda or motives.[11]

This dialogue is to be the concern of all Christians. With the pope and their bishops as guides, all local churches and all members of the Church are called upon to be involved in the dialogue in one form or the other. It is not to be reserved for experts alone or reduced to only theological discussion. It rather takes many forms and can be at different levels. For instance it takes the form of what is called "dialogue of life and faith" at which people of different religious faiths "live and work together and enrich each other through the faithful practice of the values of their various religions, without the necessity of formal discussion." This form can take place informally in the home, factory, school, college, office, hospital, village or even nation. The dialogue can take the form of "dialogue of social engagement" whose aim is the human development and liberation of human beings from environmental and social evils. In this, people of different religions cooperate in joint development projects or projects that alleviate human suffering, such as those that fight against drought, famine, poverty, ignorance, disease, violence, injustice, etc.

There is also the formal form of dialogue called "dialogue of theological discussion." in which religious or theological experts of different religions exchange views on their religions and seek understanding of each other through open-minded discussions.[12] A Christian, as a representative of the Church or Christian community, meeting in dialogue with adherents of other religions, surrenders himself to the service of God, who always directs the history of salvation. He listens to these other believers, willing to learn from them and expecting them to do the same.[13] Dialogue also includes witness to the gospel.[14] All these different forms should be seen as important and inter-connected. They are needed for dialogue to succeed.

Required of participants in inter-religious dialogue is first an interior disposition to respect the other party, to listen, to be sincere and willing to receive and to work with others. In addition, each participant should be open to the action of the Holy Spirit or God's grace which might lead him to a deeper conversion toward the will of God. Finally, he should be free to compare his religion with that of the other party, and to change his religion if he becomes convinced it is the will of God for him to do so.[15]

Reasons for the Church's Current Positive Attitude or Dialogue with Non-Christian Religions

Certain factors or reasons made the Church adopt its present friendly position or dialogical attitude toward non-Christian religions. These factors will be loosely grouped under two main subheadings, namely, sociological and theological reasons.

(a) Sociological reasons

(i) Decolonization

The twenty-five years following the Second World War was a period of rapid decolonization, especially in Africa and Asia. The new-found freedom of the peoples in these continents influenced the western world, including the hierarchy of the Catholic Church to show more respect not only to the political views of the former colonies but also to their religions and cultures.[16]

(ii) More Knowledge about Non-Christian Religions

Coinciding with the period of decolonization and possibly influenced by it was in the West an intense interest to know more about non-Christian religions. It was this interest that led Catholic theologians to study these religions in depth and to write positively about them. Many of these theologians too were consultants of the Fathers of the Second Vatican Council, the council that played, as we shall see, a far-reaching role in the Church's modification of its position on non-Christian religions. But it must be noted that the knowledge involved here is not only theoretical knowledge: it includes also knowledge of persons, of non-Christians who today have become the day-to-day neighbors of Christians and hence too close to be ignored. For experience today shows that Christians meet and work with non-Christians in many places, such as the

United Nations, in business, in offices, in institutions of learning; they live with them in the same buildings or same neighborhoods or are citizens of the same nation.[17] Furthermore, the Church came to realize that in the religious map of the world Christians constituted only a minority, roughly thirty-three percent or one third of the world population and that Catholics made up even far less than that percentage.[18] The majority of the inhabitants of the world, observes Cardinal Francis Arinze, have non-Christian religions as their way of life. And these religions "have taught generations of people how to live, how to pray, and how to die."[19] The Church therefore respects them, for over the centuries they have borne witness to man's efforts to find answers to the mysteries of life and the human condition; they are too important to be ignored today.

(iii) *Desire For Collaboration and Mutual Understanding*

By its positive attitude the Catholic Church desires to foster and to encourage others, especially Christians, to foster inter-religious collaboration both nationally and internationally. In this way, it is thought, different religions can obviate the negative tendencies that often result from inter-religious rivalry, oppression of minority groups, and the abuse of religion as a pretext for causing trouble or war.[20] Speaking to the representatives of the world religions, who at his invitation gathered at Assisi for the World Day of Prayer on October 27, 1986, Pope John Paul II said, "Either we learn to walk together in peace and harmony, or we drift apart and ruin ourselves and others."[21] The Catholic pontiff hoped that the meeting at or pilgrimage to Assisi would teach all religions again "to be aware of the common origin and destiny" of all human beings, and he urged all to see it as a symbol of fraternal love that should exist among all humans as they move toward their final destiny.[22]

Furthermore, the Church knows that when two parties of different religious persuasions meet together in a true spirit of dialogue both sides stand to gain. Not only can both sides be mutually enriched by knowing each other better, the experience can also make each side understand its beliefs better. Why? Because truth is often discovered, better appreciated and lived when met by other views. The mutual enrichment can accrue not only to individual participants in the dialogue, but also to the religions themselves. Thus from Christianity Hinayana Buddhists can learn to be more interested in social work and other initiatives toward human development. The Christian religion also can help Muslims and Buddhists to learn to give women a higher status than they have been doing. Moreover, it can show those religions that repress freedom of religion or culture how to be more tolerant. Other religions in their turn can enrich the Christian religion with their cultural settings, their "languages, philosophical categories, ritual expressions and local styles proper to their peoples".[23]

(b) Theological Reasons for the Church's Dialogical or Positive Attitude

The decisive factors for the Church's current positive attitude are, however, theological reasons. These reasons became quite cogent to the Church as a consequence of the pastoral altitude of the Second Vatican Council, the council in which, in the words of Pope John XXIII, the Church desired to present itself to the world "as the loving mother of all mankind; gentle, patient, and full of tenderness and sympathy" for all human beings both within and without the Catholic fold.[24] This was the first Catholic ecumenical council to make positive statements about non-Christian religions. Indeed, it devoted one full document, *Nostra Aetate,* to its teaching on these religions. The council thus opened the way for a more positive attitude toward non-Christian religions. Let us now see only two of the theological reasons.

(i) *Imitating the Divine Dialogue of Salvation*

The Church sees the divine dialogue of salvation as a paradigm or model it must follow. As he wanted to save mankind, God, out of pure love, initiated a dialogue between himself and man. He revealed himself gradually, adapting the revelation to the level of man's understanding until at last he made the full revelation in Jesus Christ, God and man, who revealed to men that God is love. The Church considers it its duty to continue this dialogue with other men and religions. This view was expressed by Pope Paul VI, who points out that "the dialogue of salvation was opened spontaneously on the initiative of God" because of his gratuitous love for the human race. The pope therefore considers it the duty of Christians "to take the initiative in extending to men this same dialogue without waiting to be summoned to it."[25]

And since the Church's friendly attitude, in imitation of the dialogue of salvation, is motivated by love, it excludes no one; the Church seeks sincere dialogue with all, both Christians and non-Christians, including even those who say they hate it. Especially the Second Vatican Council expresses this view. The council says that the Church in virtue of its mission on earth "shows itself as a sign of brotherhood which renders possible sincere dialogue and strengthens it." This desire to enter into sincere dialogue "excludes nobody."[26]

(ii) *Unity of the Human Race*

Thanks to the Second Vatican Council too, the Church came to understand better the unity of the human race: that all human beings have God as their common origin and final goal. Pope John Paul II underscores this truth. He points out that the unity of the human race is based on the "mystery of the divine creation:" God created all human beings and he did this in his own image. Hence there is a single plan and a common goal or destiny for every human being "whatever may be the color of his skin, the historical and geographical framework within which he happens to live and act or the culture in which he grows up and expresses himself."[27]

From what is presented above it is clear that the Catholic Church now takes its dialogue with non-Christian religions seriously. Of great interest is the realization that all human beings have the same origin and destiny, namely, God. This implies that it is God's plan that all human beings be saved (cf. 1 Tim. 2:4). The Church wishes to do whatever is possible to have this plan, the Christian economy or God's plan in Christ, realized. This is one of the Church's reasons for dialogue today. We shall see more on this topic in the chapters ahead

CHAPTER TWO

THE CHURCH AND THE JEWS

Nostra Aetate, the Second Vatican Council's declaration on the relations of the Church with non-Christian religions, marks the turning point of the relations of the Catholic Church with the Jews and Judaism.[28] In article 4, the document sets the tone of this relationship. It acknowledges the Jewish roots of the Christian religion, namely, in the patriarchs, Moses and the prophets. The document declares that all Christians are children of Abraham and that the exodus of the Jews from the land of bondage prefigures the salvation of the Church. Hence "the Church cannot forget that she received the revelation of the Old Testament" through the Jews "with whom God . . . established the old covenants". Nor does it forget "that she draws nourishment from that good olive tree onto which the wild olive branches of the Gentiles have been grafted." *Nostra Aetate* also reminds all that Jesus Christ, 'through his cross, reconciled the Jews and Gentiles and made them one in himself.'[29]

Echoing the apostle Paul in Romans 9:4-5, the same document enumerates the blessings of the Jews, including the facts that Jesus Christ was a Jew and that the apostles and members of the early Church were mainly Jews. It states that even though many of the Jews did not accept Christ and his gospel and that though some opposed the spreading of the gospel, "the Jews remain very dear to God, for the sake of the patriarchs, since God does not take back the gifts he bestowed or the choice he made." It tries to exonerate the Jews from the death of Christ, arguing that while it is true that Jewish leaders and their followers "pressed for the death of Christ . . . . neither all Jews indiscriminately at that time, nor the Jews today, can be charged with the crimes committed during his passion." It reiterates that the Church teaches that Christ, out of love, freely accepted his passion in order to free all human beings from their sins and win salvation for them.[30] In conclusion the document condemns anti-Semitism or any form of persecution against the Jews. Pointing out that the Church's current friendly attitude is motivated, not by "political consideration" but only by "Christian charity", it encourages further mutual under standing and cooperation between the Jews and Catholics, especially "by way of biblical and theological inquiry and through friendly discussions.[31] Since the publication of *Nostra Aetate* on October 28, 1965, the relationship between the Catholic Church and the Jews has improved considerably. In 1971, a committee for interaction between Catholics and the Jews was formed. This body, the International Catholic-Jewish Liaison Committee, composed of official representatives of both sides, tackles problems or questions of common interests, such as mission and proselytism, and religious freedom.[32]

The Catholic Church has continued to build up its relations with the Jews through two main channels. One of these is the Commission for Religious Relations with the Jews, and the other channel is the papacy or rather the popes. Let us now see how it functions through these two channels.

The Commission for Religious Relations with the Jews

Owing to the continued growth of the relationship between the Jews and the Catholic Church the Vatican in 1974 created a special body, the Commission for Religious Relations with the Jews, to handle its religious relations with the Jews and Judaism. This commission, linked to but distinct from, the Secretariat for Promoting Christian Unity, has, since its inauguration, played an important role in promoting Catholic-Jewish relations.[33] As the official Church organ in its relations with the Jews, it now represents the Catholic Church in the International Catholic-Jewish Liaison Committee. This commission has published a number of documents whose purpose is to improve these relations. The two most important ones published between 1974 and 1986 are, *Guidelines on the Religious Relations with the Jews* and *Notes on the Correct Way to Present the Jews and Judaism in Preaching and Catechesis in the Roman Catholic Church.* These two documents reveal how seriously the Church takes its relations with the Jews. Let us now see some aspects of the documents.

Guidelines on the Religious Relations with the Jews

The commission on January *3,* 1975 published the *Guidelines on the Religious Relations with the Jews.34* As the name indicates, the document is intended to guide Catholics in their relations with the Jews. It elaborates on article 4 of *Nostra Aetate.* outlining the nature of the Jewish-Catholic dialogue; the manner of cooperation between Jews and Catholics in the liturgy; the proper teaching or education of Catholics concerning the relations of Jews to Christians; and joint social action. With regard to authentic dialogue, it states that this has to begin immediately. First of all each side is expected to make efforts to know more about the other party and also to respect its religious convictions. Catholics, who must continue the Church's missionary activity, must maintain the strictest respect in line with the Second Vatican Council's declaration on religious liberty, *Dignitatis Humanae.* Secondly, competent representatives will meet to study together "the many problems deriving from the fundamental convictions of Judaism and of Christianity." These meetings are to be held with prayer and meditation in the presence of God.[35] Concerning the liturgy, the document stresses that, to improve the relations of the Jews and Christians, it is important to take cognizance of those common elements in the liturgical life in which the Bible holds an essential place. Reminding Catholics that the Old Testament and the New Testament are complementary to each other, it demands that in commentaries on biblical texts emphasis be laid "on the continuity of our faith with that of the earlier covenant, in perspective of promises, without minimizing those elements of Christianity which are original." Those promises, it says, were fulfilled at the first coming of Christ, though their perfect fulfillment will be at his coming at the end of time. It admonishes homilists to avoid the use of language or texts "which seem to show the Jewish people as such in an unfavorable light." The *Guidelines* directs commissions charged with the task of liturgical translations, while not altering the meaning of the text of the Bible, to be careful in phrasing those passages which can lead little-informed Christians to prejudice against the Jews.[36] As to teaching and education, after pointing out that the one and same God is the inspirer of the books of both the Old and New Testaments, the document warns that "the Old Testament and the Jewish tradition founded upon it must not be set against the New Testament" in such a way as to make the former appear only as a religion of legalism, fear, and justice, bereft of the love of God and neighbor. It dismisses as untenable any notion that maintains that Judaism is a dead religion superseded by Christianity; and directs that information concerning the Jewish tradition, the relation of the Jews to Christianity, the Jewishness of Jesus and the apostles, and other facts that will improve the Jewish-Catholic relations, be included in Catholic sources of information, especially catechism and religious books, history books, and mass media.[37] Finally, the document, just like *Nostra Aetate* before it, tries to exonerate the Jews as a people from the death of Jesus Christ. And appealing to the love of God which Jews and Christians have in common, it urges both sides to work together in the spirit of the prophets, seeking social justice and the welfare of the human person made in the image of God.[38]

Notes on the Correct Way to Present the Jews and Judaism in Preaching and Catechesis.

The *Notes on the Correct Way to Present the Jews and Judaism in Preaching and Catechesis* was published on June 24, 1985.[39] The document aims at remedying or correcting the negative ideas of most Christians about the Jews and Judaism. It discusses Judaism, the relation of the Old and New Testaments, the Messiah, and the Jewish-Christian relations, the Jewishness of Jesus, the Pharisees, the New Testament writings about the Jews, racism and anti-Semitism, the role of Israel in Jewish-Catholic dialogue, and other issues.

Recalling the statement *of Nostra Aetate* concerning the bond between the Jews and Christians, the document directs that "the Jews and Judaism should not occupy only an occasional and marginal place in catechesis" but rather should be "organically integrated" in it. Better understanding of Judaism as it is practiced today, says the document "can greatly help us to understand better certain aspects of the life of the Church." It stresses that Christian teaching about the Jews and Judaism "needs to balance a number of pairs of ideas which express the two economies of the Old and New Testaments." This means that the teacher or theologian dealing with "promise and fulfillment" has to point out that each of these two ideas lends help to the understanding of the other. In dealing with "continuity and newness," he needs to show that "newness lies in a metamorphosis of what was there before;" and with "uniqueness and exemplary nature," he needs to show respectively that "the singularity of the people of the Old Testament is not exclusive, but open, in the divine vision, to a universal extension," and that "the uniqueness of the Jewish people is meant to have the force of an example." The document did not omit pointing out the Church's duty to proclaim, in line, however, with the demands of *Dignitatis Humanae* of the Second Vatican Council, the unique and universal salvific significance of Jesus Christ.[40]

It gives a second reason for the urgency of accurate teaching about the Jews and Judaism today: it is not only to guard against the lingering remains of anti-Semitism, but rather more to instill in Christians "an exact knowledge of the wholly unique 'bond' which joins us as a church to the Jews and Judaism." This, it is hoped, will make Christians appreciate better and love the Jews who were "chosen by God to prepare the coming of Christ."[41] And the *Notes* directs the Christian teacher dealing with the relation between the

Old and New Testaments to first aim at showing the unity of the biblical revelation before he speaks of "each historical event so as to stress that particular events have meaning when seen in history as a whole." Furthermore, he should present the events of the Old Testament as concerning not only the Jews but also touching Christians personally. The Christian using typology (which the Church has applied from the apostolic and patristic times in dealing with the problem of reconciling the unity of the biblical revelation) is instructed to "be careful to avoid any transition which might seem merely a rupture" and tend toward the heresy of Marcion.[42]

It directs that the Christian applying typological reading or interpretation should keep in mind the inexhaustible riches of the Old Testament and that the New Testament be read in the background of the Old. Typology signifies progress toward the fulfillment of the divine plan of salvation which was begun in the Old Testament, now "accomplished and gradually realized by the sacraments in the church" but which will come to "its final consummation with the return of Jesus as Messiah" at the end of time. In thus stressing the eschatological character of Christianity it can become clearer that both the Jews and Christians are heading toward a similar end in the future, that is, the coming or return of the Messiah. It, therefore, behooves the people of God of the old and new covenants, that is, Jews and Christians, "to prepare the world for the coming of the Messiah by working together for social justice, respect for the rights of persons and nations and for social and international reconciliation."[43]

With profuse citation of the New Testament texts the document endeavors to authenticate the Jewish roots of Christianity. It points out that Jesus was a Palestinian Jew of the first century; that he limited his ministry to the Jews and shared the anxieties and hopes of his time and environment. He taught often in the synagogues and temple as did also his disciples even after his resurrection. Furthermore, it was "in the setting of the domestic liturgy of the Passover, or at least of the paschal festivity he intended to offer himself as a gift."[44]

After emphasizing that "the Jews" often seen in the New Testament refers to Jewish leaders or adversaries of Jesus and not Jewish people as a people, The *Notes* admits that there were conflicts between Jesus and "certain categories of Jews of his time, among them Pharisees". In addition, there was "the sad fact that the majority of the Jewish people and its authorities did not believe in Jesus." This fact intensified during the time of the early Church and led to the inevitable break or rupture between Judaism and the nascent Church. Belittling this break or overlooking it "could only prejudice the identity of either side." Yet it does not destroy the special 'bond' which *Nostra Aetate* speaks of. Here, however, the document reminds Christians that faith is a gift and that no one should judge the consciences of other people. Like *Nostra Aetate* and the *Guidelines* before it, it makes attempts to exonerate the Jews from the death of Jesus.[45]

The document points out that the Bible is the common book for the liturgy of the word in Jewish liturgy as well as in the Christian liturgy, and admits that the latter's liturgy owes much to the former. It cites as examples the liturgy of the word and the liturgy of the hours which are borrowed from the Jewish liturgy. The *Notes* laments the painful ignorance of the history and traditions of Judaism on the part of Christians, and encourages mutual knowledge of the Jewish and Christian traditions, which are closely related.[46]

These two documents, the *Guidelines* and the *Notes,* show common traits. In each there is apparent sincerity and esteem for the Jews and Judaism. They both show much concern about correcting the false ideas many Christians have about the Jews and Judaism. Each of them, just like *Nostra Aetate,* endeavors to exculpate the Jews as a people from the death of Jesus. Above all, like *Nostra Aetate* they both stress the spiritual bond between Jews and Christians and thereby acknowledge the Jewish roots of Christianity and the latter's Jewish heritage.

And on May 4, 2001, at its 17th meeting the International Liaison Committee in New York, resolved that the Catholic Church had to change how Judaism is dealt with in Catholic seminaries and schools of theology. It stated that the curricula of Catholic seminaries and schools of theology should reflect the central importance of the Church's new understanding of its relationship with the Jews and enable these institutions to know the true history and traditions of Judaism. On their part, Jewish leaders were given the task to advocate and promote a program of education in Jewish schools and seminaries about the history of the Catholic-Jewish relations and knowledge of Christianity and its relationship to Judaism. It was particularly pointed out that these institutions should especially teach about the Second Vatican Council, and subsequent documents and attitudinal changes that opened new possibilities and new ways both faiths now view each other.[47]

The Popes and Jewish-Catholic Relations

The popes that have been on the throne of Peter since 1960 have personally played very important roles in Jewish-Catholic relations. The friendly Pope John XXIII in 1960 established the Vatican Secretariat for Christian Unity, to which was to be attached later, the Commission for Religious Relations with the Jews. It was the same pope who convoked the Second Vatican Council, imparting to it his spirit of openness and dialogue, and thus setting in motion in the Church the machinery of friendly relations with the Jews and other non-Christians.

Pope Paul VI followed in the friendly footsteps of Pope John XXIII. In his very first encyclical, *Ecclesiam Suam,* he devoted several pages to his discussion on dialogue. The year 1964 saw him as the first pope in the history of the Church to make a pilgrimage to the Holy Land, where he spoke with great respect and friendliness to the Jews whom he called his brothers.[48] In 1974 he established the Commission for Religious Relations with the Jews.

Pope John Paul II carried the Jewish-Catholic relations or dialogue to its peak. Since the beginning of his pontificate there has been continuous engagement of the Vatican in efforts to let

Catholics know of the consequences of *Nostra Aetate* on the one hand, and in reaching out to the Jews on the other. Among the efforts made to make Catholics aware of the consequences of *Nostra Aetate* article 4 is the publication of the *Notes,* which we addressed above. Reaching out to the Jews has been accomplished through two main ways. One of these has been the reception in audience in the Vatican, often by the pope himself, of an enormously increased number of Jewish visitors. The other is through the pope's meetings with the Jewish community willing to meet him anywhere during his various visits throughout the world.[49] Pope John Paul II's addresses and approaches in these meetings reveal in him a spirit of sincere friendliness toward the Jews. For instance during his visit to Germany in 1980, he met in Mainz with the representatives of the Jewish community. In his address to them he insistently stated that there is a close link between the Jews and Christians. The reason for dialogue between the Jews and Christians is mainly based on this link which according to the pope has a theological implication. He saw "the faith of the church in Jesus Christ, son of David and son of Abraham" as containing "the spiritual legacy of Israel for the church." He pointed out that the depth and richness of the common inheritance of the Jews and Christians should bring them together "in friendly dialogue and mutually trustful collaboration." The pope made it clear that the Church seeks this collaboration with the Jews not simply to correct an erroneous religious view of the Jews, which in some sense contributed to the misunderstandings and persecution of the Jews; but it is above all for dialogue between the two religious bodies which together with Islam can help the world believe in the one true God.[50]

The pope discerned three dimensions of this dialogue. In two of these dimensions he stressed the continuity of the chosenness of the Jews as the people of God, pointing out that dialogue with them was like "a dialogue within our own church . . . a dialogue between the first part and the second part of the Bible." Here also he saw the task of Christians and Jews of working together for social and international peace and justice as founded on the call of Abraham to be a blessing for the world.[51] He unequivocally deplored the Nazi genocide against the Jews and its disastrous consequences. He saw them as "a tragic demonstration of where discrimination and contempt for human dignity can lead."[52]

Again, on March 6, 1982, the Roman Pontiff addressed experts in the Jewish-Christian relations, who gathered in Rome. Stressing again the bond between the Jews and Christians, he pleaded that friendliness and collaboration now replace the negative relations of the past between the two sides.[53] He also pointed out that relations with the Jews could help Christians to understand better their roots and identity. This understanding can be attained not only "by taking an inventory" of our Jewish heritage but also *"by* taking into account the faith and religious life of the Jewish people as professed and lived now."[54]

It is noteworthy that on April 13, 1986 Pope John Paul II caused a stir in the mass media of the world when he visited the main synagogue in Rome, the first pope in the history of the Church ever to visit a synagogue. His address in that unprecedented visit, though containing in essence the main ideas of the two papal addresses we just saw above, was very friendly. As usual, analyzing *Nostra Aetate* article 4, the pontiff, among other things, underscored three points: the close spiritual bond between the Jews and Christians; exoneration of the Jews from the death of Jesus; and his declaration as biblically baseless the idea which considers the Jews as cursed.[55] And in his general audience at the Vatican on April 28, 1999 the pope spoke on the Jewish-Christian dialogue in the context of the preparation for the third millennium. Here again, he recalls what Christians and Jews own in common such as common claim of Abraham as their father and the Old Testament Scripture. In view of the Jubilee of the year 2000, "which refers precisely to the Jewish tradition of jubilee years", he charges Christians and Jews to work together for peace and social justice; they are to make concerted efforts to promote "a human condition that more closely conforms to God's plan." This working together "in proclaiming and realizing God's saving plan" for all, should be marked by a courageous witness of faith. The pope hopes that at the beginning of the third millennium sincere dialogue between the Jew's and Christians "will help create a new civilization founded on the one, holy and merciful God, and fostering a humanity reconciled in love."[56]

It is to be noted that in Pope John Paul II's addresses to the Jews, he usually began on a very friendly note, expressing joy at his meeting with them. Invariably he unequivocally denounced anti-Semitism, especially as it was exhibited in the genocide against the Jews in this century. Furthermore, the pope usually quoted or cited *Nostra Aetate* article 4 and shows the implications of the statement, which include among others, the special spiritual bond between the Jews and Christians, the continuity of the chosenness of the Jews and the exoneration of the Jews from the death of Jesus.

From what we have seen so far in the activities of the Commission for Religious Relations with the Jews and the popes since the Second Vatican Council, it is evident that *the* Catholic Church sincerely desires friendly relations with the Jews. Among the signs of progress are the continual meetings in different parts of the world of the International Catholic-Jewish Liaison Committee. Progress in the relationship between the two sides has been steady because they have continued to work together with sincerity, mutual esteem and love—dispositions which are vital for genuine dialogue. These dispositions, for instance, dominated when the liaison committee met on September 3-6, 1990 in Prague. In a joint statement the committee declared, "As Catholics and Jews we have a sacred duty to strive to create after two millennia of estrangement and hostility a genuine culture of mutual esteem and reciprocal caring." A gesture of this caring is the joint recommendation made by the committee as to the way to uproot anti-Semitism, especially in central and eastern Europe where the collapse of communism has revealed or rekindled old ethnic rivalries (as was, for instance, recently seen between the Serbs and ethnic Albanians). The Catholic delegation independently denounced anti-Semitism and all forms of racism as a sin against God and humanity.[57] Although anti-Semitism still exists in places, the contemporary Catholic attitude has put on the defensive those who still maintain this attitude. In other words, the Catholic Church has shown clearly that it is against this evil, and everyone who is still involved in it is working against the wishes and desires of the Catholic Church. In addition, a certain amount of trust in the Church has been generated in the Jews.[58]

Despite this progress, however, the Church has encountered a number of challenges in its relations with the Jews. There were two main sources of problems in the Church's dialogue with the Jews and Judaism. One of these was the insistence by the Jews that the Church have diplomatic relations with the state of Israel. The other was the presence of a Carmelite convent near the former Nazi concentration camp at Auschwitz, where about two million Jews died, a place the Jews regard as sacred to them. The challenges posed by these two sources have been overcome since the desired diplomatic relations have been established (as we shall show below) and the convent has been relocated in a different site. Yet, new problems continue to arise. The lingering one is the continued accusation of some Jews that the silence of Pope Pius XII made it easier for the Nazi persecutors to kill many Jews, an accusation the Catholic Church has consistently denied. Catholics cite a number of facts which show that the pope did much to save the Jews from Nazism during the Holocaust. Among these facts is the *New York Times* editorial for Christmas 1941 which praised the pope for confronting Hitler and making it clear that the aims of Nazism were contrary to Christian peace. Another one is the statement credited to a one-time prime minister of Israel Golda Meir, which also praised the pope for saving many lives by speaking out against Nazism. The pope is said to be responsible for saving at least seven hundred thousand Jews. This made the chief rabbi of Rome then to convert to the Catholic faith.[59] In his Italian-language version of the book *Pius XII and the Second World War,* the Vatican's leading expert on the Second World War maintains that the pope sometimes applied silent diplomacy which he said helped the pontiff to save the Jews quietly through nunciatures and episcopates.[60] However, despite all efforts made by the Catholic Church to convince the Jews that Pope Pius XII did his best to save the Jews during the Second World War, they still see him as a collaborator of the Nazis in the Holocaust (or Nazi attempt to destroy all the Jews) and are strongly opposed to his beatification or canonization. Their hatred for him presents a strong stumbling block on the road of the Catholic—Jewish dialogue. For instance, at the beginning of his pontificate when Pope Benedict XVI visited a Cologne synagogue in 2005 the head of the Jewish community there insisted that he open all Vatican archives connected with World War II so the public might know the role played by Pius XII during that war.

It has been observed that by allowing Moslems to build a mosque near the Basilica of the Annunciation in Nazareth, the site where Christians believe the Archangel Gabriel announced to the Virgin Mary that she would be the mother of Jesus, the state of Israel raised a new problem not only for the dialogue between the Church and the Jews but also for the relations between the Church and Moslems. In protest, Christians closed their churches on the two days that the building of the mosque would commence. The unrest caused by this friction threatened to spoil the 2000 Jubilee celebration in Nazareth.[61]

And in January 2009, the president of the Vatican Council for Justice and Peace, Cardinal Renato Marino's criticism of Israel's offensive in the Hamas-ruled Gaza strip drew the anger of Israel. As a response, the chief rabbi of Venice, Elia Enrico Richetti, announced his boycott of the Church's annual celebration of Judaism.[62]

However, the Catholic Church is not deterred in its determination to promote good relationship with the Jews. And it is now understood that what gives the Jewish-Catholic relationship much strength is the realization by both sides that this relationship has a theological basis, especially the spiritual bond which has been mentioned several times. This makes the relations of the Church with the Jews and Judaism, among non-Christians, special. Pope John Paul II during his historic visit to Rome's main synagogue in 1986, underscored this special relationship with these words: "The Jewish religion is not 'extrinsic' to us, but in a certain way 'intrinsic' to our religion. With Judaism therefore we have a relationship which we do not have with any other religion."[63] It is no surprise therefore that the Vatican Commission for Religious Relations with the Jews is linked to, though distinct from, the Secretariat for Christian Unity and not to the Secretariat for Inter-religious Dialogue. Yet, the Church always insists that this friendly approach should not be confused with religious relativism or a loss of identity on the part of the Church which without equivocation professes its faith in the universal significance of the paschal mystery, the death and resurrection of Jesus Christ.[64]

The steady progress made in the Jewish-Catholic relations led to a diplomatic agreement at Jerusalem on December 30, 1993 between the Vatican and the State of Israel. This agreement, titled "Fundamental Agreement between the Holy See and the State of Israel", signed by Msgr. Claudio Celli for the Vatican and Yossi Beilin, Israel's deputy minister for foreign affairs for Israel would lead to full diplomatic relations between the two sovereign states. The agreement called for the exchange of diplomatic envoys, and clearly stated that full diplomatic relations would be established after the ratification of the agreement[65] On June 15, 1994 the Vatican and the State of Israel announced the establishment of full diplomatic relations and exchange of ambassadors. As noted by the Vatican, this new relationship would provide a better opportunity for more dialogue between the Church and the State of Israel. It would also help the Church to defend Jerusalem and the Holy Land as "unique historic, cultural and religious patrimony." This was a very important milestone in the Christian-Jewish dialogue.[66] Indeed it has taken that dialogue to a very great height and many more good results are expected to come from there. Pope John Paul II's March 20-26, 2000 pilgrimage to the Holy Land, which was also the first official papal visit to the state of Israel, is one of the good results that can come from this friendly relationship. That visit was much appreciated by the Jews. Speaking after the pope's Mass by the Sea of Galilee on March 24, 2000 the Israeli Prime Minister Ehud Barak noted that the pope's visit was "a major step toward reconciliation between the Jewish people and Christianity." It will play an important role not only in the dialogue between Christians and Jews but also in the overall peace of the Middle East.[67]

CHAPTER THREE

THE CHURCH'S GENERAL RELATIONS WITH OTHER NON-CHRISTIAN RELIGIONS

The Catholic Church has also built up good relations, or at least is disposed to have such good relations, with other non-Christian religions. But treating in detail the relations of the Church with every one of these religions (which are very many and some have multiple families[68]) is beyond the scope of this book. In this chapter, we shall present the Catholic Church's general plans for dialogue or friendly relations with every sincere non-Christian religion.

The General Arrangements for Dialogue or Friendly Relations with Non-Christians: Vatican Secretariat for Inter-religious Dialogue and Its Arms.

In 1964 the Vatican set up the Secretariat for inter-religious Dialogue (formerly known as the Secretariat for Non-Christians) as an institutional symbol of the Catholic Church's sincerity for dialogue or good relations with non-Christian religions. The task of the secretariat is to promote dialogue between the Church and non-Christian religions. Most bishops' conferences too have commissions or offices, or at least persons whose duty is to engage in a similar task. According to their general needs and capabilities, dioceses are also expected to take a similar step. Apart from all these, continental or area bishops' conferences have commissions or offices whose task is to promote dialogue with non-Christians. For instance, the Federation of Asian Bishops' Conference has a permanent office at Taipei, Taiwan, for ecumenical and inter-religious affairs, which office has set up at least four bishops' institutes for inter-religious affairs with Buddhism, Islam, and Hinduism; organized several seminars on inter-religious affairs: and has made plans to organize a seminar each year for bishops of the area, so that within a period of about six years every bishop in the Asian continent will attend at least one inter-religious seminar.[69]

The secretariat itself creates forums for encounters between Christians and non-Christians by organizing in various countries inter-religious meetings or encounters. For example, from 1974 to 1978, it organized such encounters in Cairo (twice), Luxemburg, Bangkok, Bamako (Mali), Abidjan (Ivory Coast), Kampala (Uganda), Niamey (Niger), Tripoli (Libya), Yaoundé (Cameroon), Kyoto, Vienna, Praglia, Tokyo, Nemi (Japan). It also encourages local churches and other bodies to organize similar encounters in which it participates. Such encounters have been organized by the Asian Bishops' Institute on Inter-religious Affairs at Bangkok (1979 and 1984), Kualalumpur (1979), Madras (1982). From 1980 to 1984 the local churches also organized encounters annually at Arras. Centre d' Etudes des Religions Africaines has organized in Kinshasa (Congo) two encounters, one being a colloquium on African spirituality (1978 and 1983).[70]

Furthermore, the secretariat easily accepts invitations to participate in inter-religious meetings or encounters organized by other bodies, be they Christian or non-Christian. Examples of such meetings are those organized by the World Religionists Ethics Congress: God-man-nature at Tokyo (1981); Journees Romaines (1981, 1983); Islamo-Christian Congress in Rome (1981); congress at Cochin (1982): encounters at Assisi (1982) and Al-Azhar (1983). Many similar meetings or encounters took place especially in 1984: Theological Inter-religious Convention in Padua; meeting of World Inter-monastic Aid Committee in Paris; first International Summer Institute for Islamic Studies at Marawi, Philippines; World Conference on Religion and Peace at Nairobi; Commission on Islam of the Episcopal Conferences of Francophone West Africa at Abidjan;

Asian Bishops' Institute on Inter-religious Affairs at Sampran, Bangkok; Consultation on Islamo-Christian-Jewish Dialogue at Windsor, England; Mediterranean International Convention on Christianity and Islam at Palermo.[71]

In addition to all these, there are many other encounters, congresses, and meetings in different parts of the world which various officials of the secretariat participate in and often deliver, on behalf of the secretariat, important addresses, conduct workshops, and give information about the secretariat and the Church to others.[72]

But the secretariat is not working alone as can be seen above: it has the cooperation of some non-Christian bodies; of the Dialogue of People of Living Faiths and Ideologies; above all, of regional and national episcopal conferences. Most of the conferences or encounters are indeed organized by the local churches, which shows that dialogue is not the concern of the Secretariat for Inter-religious Dialogue alone or the Vatican only: it is the concern of the whole Church. It is, in fact, in the levels of the local church, that is, at the diocesan, national, regional and continental levels that the Catholic Church meets the believers of non-Christian religions at the grassroots level. There are now at least sixty commissions for inter-religious dialogue at these different levels set up by the bishops' conferences.[73]

The churches in Asia and Africa, the two continents which have a majority of non-Christians, are making great efforts to foster inter-religious dialogue and a better understanding of the various cultures of the peoples (which are usually influenced by the predominant religion). Worthy of special mention for these positive efforts are the Federation of Asian Bishops' Conferences, and the Regional Bishops' Conference of Francophone West Africa. But, as noted in chapter one of this book, non-Christians today are not confined to Africa and Asia: many of them now live in North America and Europe. Many churches in these areas also promote dialogue with the non-Christians among them.[74]

These efforts of the Church have surely yielded some positive results. But the Church has also encountered a lot of difficulties or challenges in its undertaking. We shall here highlight a few of both the progress and the challenges.

Progress

The general result of the Church's friendly gesture is goodwill or good relations or easing of the tension between the Church and non-Christians religions. A good illustration of this is the response of all the main religions of the world to Pope John Paul II's invitation that their representatives gather in Assisi on October 27, 1986, for prayer for inter-religious peace. All known religious traditions had representatives at this encounter. Together these religious leaders fasted, together they meditated, and together they walked for inter-religious peace. Each religious tradition or group prayed in turn while the other religious traditions watched with keen interest: each religion prayed separately. Addressing the representatives on the occasion, Pope John Paul II noted that that gathering was the first time that different religious traditions, both Christian and non-Christian from all over the world, had come together to "witness before the world, each according to his own conviction, about the transcendent peace." Although the form and content of the prayers were different, yet in that very difference they "have perhaps discovered anew that, regarding the problem of peace and its relation to religious commitment, there is something which binds us together".[75] That which binds them together is the quest for peace which is to be promoted by sincere dialogue and prayer.[76]

There are also illustrations of the goodwill seen in individual religious traditions. It is owing to it that non-Christian heads of state now invite the Pope to visit their countries and often in times of great need go to him for consultation or advice. For instance, the king of Morocco invited Pope John Paul II to his country to address over eighty thousand Moslem youths on August 19, 1985.[77] And in September 1999, after signing the West Bank land-for-security treaty with Israel, the Palestinian leader Yasser Arafat hurried to Italy to discuss the accord with Pope John Paul II.[78] In addition, there are more visits of non-Christian leaders to Catholic leaders. Here are a few examples. The exiled Dalai Lama of Tibet visited the Vatican in 1973, 1980, and 1982; the Buddhist patriarch of Thailand did the same in 1972 and that of Laos in 1973. These religious leaders are usually granted papal audience. Catholic leaders especially from the Secretariat for Inter-religious Dialogue also visit non-Christian countries and institutions.[79] Owing to the same reason non-Christians now comfortably attend Catholic liturgy. An example is the case of the Romanesque Cathedral of Saint Louis in Missouri where many Moslems and Jews joined Pope John Paul II and other Catholics in the evening prayer on January 27, 1999, during the pope's visit there.[80]

Especially in Japan there are growing interests in Christianity among non-Christians and they have great esteem for the pope, which some of them show by following the direction of the Church in their search for ideals. For instance, in his 1983 acceptance speech in Rome on receiving the Artisan Peace Prize, a prominent Japanese Buddhist, Nikkyo Niwano, said to the pope; "I am moved, Your Holiness, because this prize is nothing but the consequence of my activity, as a Buddhist naturally, in following the teaching of Vatican II."[81] Many Japanese non-Christians now visit Rome often. Some of them even venerate the grave of Cardinal Pignedoli, former president of the Secretariat for Non-Christians. And thirty Japanese Buddhist youths were in Rome in 1984 to join the youth jubilee of the Holy Year. Furthermore, there has been inter-monastic dialogue between Catholic monks and Japanese Buddhist monks. This is done by exchange of monks for some weeks. Thus some Catholic monks live with Buddhist monks in the latter's monastery for some four weeks. And Buddhist monks do the same in Catholic monasteries.[82]

Challenges

Despite the successes we have seen, there are still many and serious challenges facing the Church in its effort to promote friendly relations with non-Christian religions. Only a few of these problems, or rather challenges, will be briefly treated in these pages. Here they are.

Confusion in Understanding the Church's Stand

The fact that the Catholic Church simultaneously takes seriously both its dialogue with non-Christians and the proclamation of the gospel seems to cause some confusion among many Catholics. Cardinal Krol made this observation as early as 1974, during the synod of bishops that year. He noted that the Church's friendly attitude was causing some confusion in evangelization, for it seemed to many Catholics that the Church had substituted inter-religious dialogue for the proclamation of the gospel.[83]

Pope Paul VI in *Evangelii Nuntiandi* also laments the fact that some confusion or difficulty has arisen owing to a misunderstanding by some people of the Second Vatican Council's teaching concerning evangelization and dialogue. The pontiff sees the problem as "complex and all the more serious because it arises from within." He regrets the loss of interest, joy and hope in many evangelizers whose excuses have arisen from insidious insinuations "which are allegedly based on this or that teaching of the council."[84]

Identification of Christianity with the West

Many non-Christian religions (which are mostly in Asia and Africa) often identify Christianity with the Western world. Hence they usually give the Church some share of the blame or grievances they have against the greed, lust for power, and insensitivity to human suffering of Western political and economic powers. An illustration of this was the Persian Gulf War of 1990. It was observed then that the war damaged or at least lessened the prospects for dialogue soon between Christians, Jews, and Moslems. For, even though several Arab nations joined the American-led coalition, and despite the fact that Pope John Paul II appealed in vain many times to both Saddam Hussein and George Bush (the leaders of Iraq and the United States) to look for a solution to the crisis through peaceful negotiations, many Moslems regarded that war as a crusade, a Christian holy war against Moslems. This observation was made by Catholic prelates from different parts of the Middle East in the meeting the pope held between March 4 to 6, 1991 with representative bishops from all the countries involved in the Persian Gulf War.[85]

And in Africa the scandal of the transatlantic slave trade and the European partition and colonization of the continent were and still are big obstacles to many people embracing Christianity whole-heartedly. These people see the West as the main cause of the woes of Africa today, maintaining that before the Westerners introduced into the continent their insensitivity to human suffering greed and lust for power, Africa had its own industries, was as prosperous as the most developed parts of Europe and that Africans traded on equal terms with Europeans. This accusation may look exaggerated. But those who hold fast to it give us more information to make their case clearer. They cite as an example the encounter of Nigeria with Europeans or the West.

The first Europeans to visit Nigeria were the Portuguese who came about the year 1472. Nigerians' articles of trade with them and other Europeans were pepper, ivory and locally-made textiles which were much in demand in Europe. Later, however, when the New World was discovered with its potential of wealth, especially in mineral resources, there was great need for human labor. The native Indians died in great numbers partly because the work was too hard for them and partly from the diseases transmitted by Europeans. Europeans had to turn to Nigeria and other West African countries for human labor. To their great joy there were in West Africa insensitive collaborators who were ready to hunt for and capture human beings for sale. And here was the dawn of the transatlantic slave trade. In 1518 the first load of slaves was sent to the West Indies. This trade was to last for three centuries and millions of Africans were uprooted from their homes and sold as slaves to Europeans. Europe or rather the West and their industries gained heavily at the expense of Africa, its inhabitants and industries.[86]

Young and old people alike, including even pregnant women, were captured or kidnapped, usually in their homes or neighborhoods while carrying out their normal duties, visiting some friends or alone at home. For instance, Olaudah Equino, while eleven years old, was kidnapped with his sister while they were alone at home and sold to European slavers.[87] The captives suffered indescribable hardships and humiliation. To put it briefly, they were treated not as human beings but as wild beasts. Barely clothed and half-starved, they were sold at slave fairs in the hinterland and walked long distances to the coast, chained to one another to prevent them from escaping. They passed through several hands and were ultimately sold to European slavers at Bonny, Calabar, Elim Kalabari and other ports. Owing to the inhuman treatment they were subjected to, many of the slaves died on their way to the ports or inside slave ships.[88] Wars were big sources of slaves; for many of these wars were indeed connected with or provoked by the trade. Some were waged as a reprisal for an act of abduction, others with the pure intention of capturing human beings for sale. White slavers usually supplied the arms and ammunition.

The corrupting effect of the slave trade was soon evident as the trade continued among Nigerians (and other Africans). This effect was especially disregard for human dignity and life, particularly the dignity and life of Africans. Even among Nigerians/Africans themselves the value of human dignity fell so low that communities started to sell their own people whom they considered to be criminals. And amazingly, even among Nigerians (who generally love large families), some family members sometimes sold their relatives, and friends betrayed friends. There were suspicion and uncertainty everywhere, and hardly could anyone trust any other person.[89]

This disregard for human life remained with Nigerians and other Africans even after the abolition of the slave trade in the nineteenth century. After this abolition, African slave traders did not know what to do with the slaves they had. To dispose of these slaves, they resorted to human sacrifice. Slaves were killed as a mark of honor at the burial of great men. Thus were forty slaves killed at the burial of Obi Ossai, king of Aboh who died about 1845.[90]

The miseries and setbacks created by the slave trade are innumerable. Not only were Nigeria and the continent of Africa as a whole impoverished and depopulated, not only was the social life disrupted and crippling fear cast into the psyche and minds of most Africans owing to this infernal trade, the African and every black person is often looked upon by many as an inferior, sub-human creature, who does not count much.[91]

Nor were the slave trade and its concomitants all that Africans had to suffer from their contacts with the West. The crises generated by the slave trade merged with another crisis: colonization of the continent by Europeans. This was not an easy task for the colonizers who had to use force to effect their plans. In Nigeria, for example, the British government initiated its colonization of Igbo land with violence and Igbo people had to resist it for more than twenty years.[92] The clashes became more violent from 1885 when the Royal Niger Company gained a Charter to govern. The company blockaded the city of Onitsha which refused to cooperate with its policy of monopoly of trade, fought Obosi, and destroyed half of Asaba town. In 1892 it was locked in a bitter war with Aguleri town; and because of the similarity of the sound of the name of Aguleri and Umeleri, it attacked the latter. In these colonizing wars the colonizers often enlisted to fight on their side Africans from the territories they had already captured or occupied. So was the case in the struggle to capture Igboland. Here the British enlisted a large number of Africans from the Gold Coast, Yorubaland and Housaland to fight on their side. Thus in the Arochukwu expedition which lasted from

December 1901 to March 1902, the British forces consisted of 74 white officers and 3464 African soldiers and carriers.[93]

The miseries brought on Nigerians and other Africans were similar and of equal magnitude to those brought by the slave trade. The British, especially, were ruthless toward the towns that resisted. Sometimes it was not enough for them to kill as many people as they could; they further razed to the ground all the buildings in a town and destroyed all the fruit trees and plants in the farms thus leaving for the people neither shelter nor food. Many people were rendered homeless and forced to flee their towns. Two Catholic stations at Nsugbe and Aguleri at one time had fifteen thousand refugees.[94] Even women were not spared in the massacre. For instance, the British troops fired at women in the Aba Women's Riot of 1929-1930, killing 55 and wounding 50.[95]

It is clear from these few lines that the coming of the slave trade and the colonization which closely followed on its heels looted the natural and human resources of Africa, scattered families, badly depopulated the continent, and destroyed African industries, sending the continent hundreds of years back in its progress and inflicted almost incurable trauma and other evils on Africans and people of African descent in different parts of the world today. Making little or no distinction between Christianity (which came to most Africans from the West) and Western socio-economic and political powers, many Africans do not wish to enter into dialogue with the church and they question how Westerners who were the causes of their woes can preach to them about a God who is good and just. It is not usually an easy task for the missionary or evangelizer to explain the difference between the Western economic and political powers and the Church. And often unless this explanation is properly given and accepted, the Christian message is not acceptable by many Africans.

And in Asia, especially in China, one of the main obstacles to evangelization since the nineteenth century is that the missionaries or evangelizers are viewed with suspicion and associated with European or American colonial expansionism.[96]

Divided Christianity

The divisions between Christian denominations and the continuous proliferation of churches pose problems for both evangelization and dialogue. For these divisions cause some confusion and scandal to non-Christians, since each Christian denomination claims to be the true church of Christ. This fact is a source of grief for the Catholic Church, especially since the time of the Second Vatican Council. The council notes with deep regret that "such division openly contradicts the will of Christ, scandalizes the world, and damages the most holy cause, the preaching of the Gospel to every creature."[97] *Evangelii Nuntiandi* makes a similar observation with the following words: "The division now existing among Christians is a very grave state of affairs which is impeding the work of Christ."[98]

Dialogue also shares in the problem raised by this division. The fact that Christians cannot speak with one voice often puts their seriousness to doubt before non-Christians. To make things worse, some fundamentalist groups that claim to be Christian often proselytize without respect to human freedom and dignity, thus annoying non-Christians and putting dialogue in jeopardy.[99]

CHAPTER FOUR

THE CHURCH'S RELATIONS WITH ISLAM, BUDDHISM, HINDUISM, AND TRADITIONAL RELIGION

In this chapter we shall consider some of the Church's efforts in the promotion of dialogue with a few individual major world religions, namely, Islam, Hinduism, Buddhism, and African Traditional Religion. However, the relations, as presented below, are to be seen only as samples of the Church's goodwill or desire for friendly relations with all sincere non-Christian religions.

(i) The Church and Islam

The Church's relations with Moslems have been mentioned several times before. With Moslems and Jews, Christians believe in one God, mankind's judge at the end of time; and each of these religions links its faith to the faith of the patriarch Abraham. The relations of the Church with Moslems started changing for the better from the Second Vatican Council when the Church discovered and praised the qualities in Islam, the religion of Moslems. Apart from the positive way Moslems are described in article 16 of *Lumen Gentium,* the council in article 3 of *Nostra Aetate* enumerates the reasons why the Church today holds Moslems in high esteem. These reasons include the fact that they worship the one, living, subsistent, merciful and almighty God, "the creator of heaven and earth who has spoken to men." They, like Abraham to whose faith they link their own, submit themselves to the hidden plans of God; they venerate Mary, the mother of Jesus, and Jesus himself whom they accept as a prophet, though not as God; and they look forward to the resurrection of the dead, God's judgment and reward on the last day. Owing to this expectation they hold in high regard "an upright life and worship of God, especially by way of prayer, alms-deeds and fasting."[100] Taking cognizance of these positive traits and the closeness of Moslems to Christians, the Church pleads with both Moslems and Christians to forget their past hostile relations and to work seriously together to "preserve and promote peace, liberty, social justice and moral values."[101]

Some progress has been made. Since 1967 the Secretariat for Inter-religious Dialogue has been sending a good-will message every year to Moslems during their most sacred time of Ramadan. Moslems usually write back to acknowledge their acceptance of the messages. The intensive efforts of the same Secretariat has made it possible for its officers to visit religious leaders in Islamic countries, such as Saudi Arabia, Iraq, Iran, Egypt, Pakistan, Libya, Indonesia, and Jordan. By the same token these leaders have also visited the Vatican. And usually Moslem leaders are given a warm welcome at the Vatican. A few examples can illustrate this. The secretariat in March 1984 organized in the Pontifical Gregorian University a conference on behalf of the Egyptian undersecretary of state. And in September 1984 an audience with the pope was given to Dr. D. Omar Naceef, secretary general of the World Arab League. In addition to this, the ambassadors of Islamic nations accredited to the Vatican often visit the secretariat.[102] There is now a colloquium every two years organized by the Pontifical Secretariat for Interreligious Dialogue and the Tehran-based Center for Interreligious Dialogue of the Islamic Culture and Relations Organization. This takes place alternately between Rome and Tehran. For instance, the sixth colloquium took place in Rome in April 2008. The seventh session took place in November 2010 in Tehran, Iran. In this session participants agreed that faith, by its nature, requires freedom and that hence religious freedom must be respected by individuals, society and the state. This colloquium was filled with friendly atmosphere.[103]

This good rapport is yielding positive diplomatic results. Thanks to it the Vatican and the Islamic State of Bahrain in the Persian Gulf have now agreed to establish diplomatic relations.[104] And on February 14, 2000 the Vatican and the Palestinian Liberation Organization signed an agreement which called for an internationally guaranteed statute for Jerusalem to make it easy to protect basic religious freedoms in that holy city. This agreement termed "Basic Agreement" rejects and sees as morally wrong and legally unacceptable "unilateral decisions and actions altering the specific character and status of Jerusalem." It rather expresses the view that "an equitable solution for the issue of Jerusalem, based on international resolutions, is fundamental for a just and lasting peace for the Middle East." It calls for a negotiated Middle East Peace agreement that would "realize the inalienable national legitimate rights and aspirations of the Palestinians." This agreement has been described as the most significant development in the Vatican's relations with the Palestinian Liberation Organization since the official ties were established in 1994.[105]

Challenges in the Dialogue with Moslems

Though some progress has been made in the Church's relations with Moslems, yet there are still a lot of challenges. The first challenge is that many Moslem leaders do not want to sit in dialogue with Christians or the Jews. Two examples here can illustrate this. One was the attitude of Moslem leaders of Nigeria when Pope John Paul II visited that nation in 1982. Just a few hours before their scheduled meeting with the pontiff, they cancelled it without giving any reason for their action.[106] Another one was at the special inter-religious meeting arranged at the Notre Dame center in Jerusalem during Pope John Paul II's visit to the Holy Land in March 2000. The local Moslem leader, the *mufti* of Jerusalem refused to attend because the Israeli chief rabbi would be in attendance. And the Moslem representative walked out of the gathering when he saw young members of Jewish, Christian, and Moslem choirs joined together in song.[107]

Another challenge comes from the different ways Christians and Moslems view human beings and human freedom. Thanks to their knowledge of Christ, the incarnation and the paschal mystery, Christians know human beings not only as persons made in the image and likeness of God, but also as sons and daughters of God and brothers and sisters of Christ. Hence they show love to all because of their love of God and the high position they know a human person has in the eyes of God. For this reason too they allow everyone freedom of worship, so that in matters of religion or belief no one or group is coerced to act against their conscience: all have within reasonable limits freedom of association in these matters.[108] Moslems on the other hand see the human person only as a slave of God. For them to call a human person a son or daughter of God is an insult or blasphemy against God who is too transcendent to be called father of any human being. A human being is always a slave of God and remains so even if elevated to be God's agent or ambassador in the world. This low esteem in which Moslems hold a human person makes them have comparatively little respect for human rights and freedom. And since they do not see much separation between politics and religion, Moslem governments in Africa and Asia often oppress the Christians and try to force them to become Moslems, usually by imposing on all citizens, Moslems and non-Moslems alike, the *shariah* or Moslem way of life. This was the case, for example, in Nigeria during the Moslem dictatorship of Ibrahim Babangida and Sani Abacha, when Moslems did all they could to impose the Moslem way of life on all Nigerians and even registered that country into the Organization of Islamic Conference, even though Moslems did not constitute more than half the population. Christians there were also oppressed in various other ways.[109] It was the same attitude that made some Nigerian states that were predominantly Moslem declare the *shariah* in their areas in the early months of the year 2000, which triggered off riots that claimed thousands of lives especially of Christians living in Moslem territories. The Pope in his World Day of Peace message for 1991, which was released in the Vatican on December 8, 1990, spoke against religious intolerance. The statement, as was observed, was directed especially to Moslems who try to impose their religion on other people.[110] And even in Europe today it is observed that Moslems are threatening to invade Christians there. One such observation was made in 1999 by Archbishop Giussepe Bernardini of Smyrna, Turkey, owing to hostile statements publicly made by prominent Moslem figures during Christian-Moslem meetings. The prelate noted that instead of using the huge amount of money from the oil sales to create jobs for the countries of North Africa and the Middle East, Moslems use this money to construct new mosques and cultural centers in Christian countries and cities including even Rome.[111] Despite these unfriendly attitudes of Moslems the Catholic Church has continued to show friendly gestures to them all. For instance at the dawn of Jubilee 2000 Cardinal Francis Arinze, in his message to Moslems, said that the Catholic Church wants to help the latter "to be associated with" the Great Jubilee of Christianity.[112]

Partly thanks to the efforts of the Secretariat for inter-religious Dialogue in various states or countries the relations between Christians and Moslems have improved much. This is the case in some Islamic states of North Africa, where Christians and Moslems live quietly together. In Asia, there is mutual understanding between Christians and Moslems in some countries; dialogue continues between Christians and Moslems in the Philippines, India, Bangladesh, and Pakistan. Moslems living in Europe and North America enjoy freedom of worship.[113]

Pope John Paul II and Catholic-Moslem Relations

Pope John Paul II consistently showed his interest in the growth of the relations between Catholics and Moslems. In his journeys around the world, he met with representatives of the Moslem community where there were Moslems willing to meet with him. In these meetings the pope usually endeavored to point out what Christians and Moslems have in common, such as belief in one God. One example is the pope's address on August 19, 1985, to about eighty thousand Moslem youths from different parts of the Arab world who gathered at Casablanca, Morocco, for the Pan-Arab games. Early in that address, the pope told the youths that Catholics and Moslems have many things in common as human beings and as believers in God. As human beings both Christians and Moslems live in the same world, a world that is "marked by numerous signs of hope but also many signs of anguish." As believers, who have Abraham as their model, both Christians and Moslems believe in the one and only living God, the creator of the worlds and all that are in them. This same God who is the origin of all life, and is also "the source of all that is good, all that is beautiful, all that is holy," wants all of us to respect every human being, "love him as a friend, a companion, a brother", to help him "when he is hurt, when he is abandoned, when he is hungry"; in short when he is in need. We are responsible for all our actions to the same God, whom we love and adore, and who is not only our truly merciful but also just judge. [114]

Summarizing the contents of *Nostra Aetate,* especially the third article, the pontiff said his coming to meet with the Moslems was in the spirit of this Second Vatican Council document, in which the Church committed itself to seek collaboration among believers. For Moslems and Christians, he stressed, this collaboration or dialogue as well as joint witness to God "in a world which is becoming more and more secularized, at times even atheistic", is more necessary today than ever. As believers, both Christians and Moslems must give witness to the spiritual values which the world needs today. These include worship of God, "prayer of praise and supplication," and search for God's will. This witness, the pope, however, emphasized, must respect other religious traditions, "for every man expects to be respected for what he is in fact and what he believes in conscience, free from external constraints" unworthy of human dignity. And no one can truly pray to God the creator of all human beings, when he does not treat other human beings with respect and love. Therefore respect, love, and help to every human being, who is God's creature, his image, his representative and the way that leads to him, are necessary for authentic belief in God; they also favor dialogue and hence peace and understanding among peoples.[115]

The pope challenged those Moslem youths to combine love, self-discipline and collaboration with others, old and young alike, to fight the ills of the world: racism, misunderstanding, wars, injustice, joblessness, etc., and therefore to build a better world, a world of the twenty-first century, which he said was in the hands of the youth. He compared the world to a living body in which the different parts co-exist by a process of co-dependence. The failure to respect this fact, he pointed out, had bedeviled the world with division, conflicts and injustices. He charged, especially the youths of Morocco, a nation that has a long "tradition of openness," and which has been a meeting point for many civilizations, "to build a civilization founded on love" of all human beings, hence tearing down "barriers which are sometimes caused by pride."[116]

Concluding the pope declared: "The Catholic Church respects and recognizes the quality of your religious approach, the richness of your spiritual tradition. We Christians are also proud of our religious tradition." He prayed that God might one day enlighten Moslems and Christians on the mystery of Jesus Christ of Nazareth, belief in whom or lack of it is the main difference between the two religious traditions.[117]

The pontiff's love for Moslems was made even clearer during his pilgrimage and journey to the Middle East in the early months of the year 2000. In his sermon at a public Mass in Egypt he exhorted both Christians and Moslems, while respecting their different religious views, to place their skills at the service of the nation for the welfare of their country. He pointed out that the Church-run charitable and social agencies were open to all, both Christians and Moslems.[118] In Jordan the pope praised the efforts of King Abdullah II to promote tolerance and peace in the Middle East. He called attention to the problems of the Palestinians forced out of their homes by past wars.

These problems he saw as "grave and urgent issues of justice, of the rights of peoples and nations which have to be resolved for the good of all concerned and as a condition for lasting peace." He urged all concerned to seek for peace no matter how difficult and how long it would take. The pope praised the tradition of religious freedom in predominantly Moslem Jordan and wished that his visit would "strengthen the already fruitful Catholic-Muslim dialogue" in that country. He later met with the king to discuss inter-religious matters and the prospects of peace in the Middle East.[119] In his own speech at the airport, King Abdullah II called Pope John Paul II "a symbol of all that is pure and noble in this life," and said that the pope had already brought a "light of hope by visiting the region and had served the cause of peace" by reminding the people of the need for faith and forgiveness of one's enemies.[120]

At Bethlehem, which is occupied by Palestinians, the Holy Father expressed his regrets that the Palestinians had suffered for very long. He made it clear that the Holy See had always recognized the natural rights of the Palestinian people for a homeland and to live in peace and harmony. He reiterated that there could be no lasting peace in the Holy Land without a stable guarantee for the rights of all involved "on the basis of international law and the relevant United Nations resolutions and declarations." The pope added, "The promise of peace will become reality for the world only when the dignity and rights of all human beings made in the image of God are acknowledged and respected." At the United Nations-run camp school, the pope expressed his sympathy with the refugees who had been deprived of proper healthcare, housing, education, work, freedom, the closeness of relatives and familiar surroundings as well as their cultural traditions. He admonished them not to think that their current conditions made them less in the sight of God. The pope reminded them that when Jesus, the God-man, first came into the world he was born at Bethlehem in humility and poverty and that the good news of his birth was first announced to the poor, the shepherds. The pontiff promised that the Church, through its charitable and social organizations, would continue to help the

Palestinians and to plead their cause before the world.[121] The pope's sincerity and love for Moslems is thus clear.

In his visit to Kazakhstan, a country with a large Moslem population, in September 2001, the pope again publicly affirmed the Church's respect for Islam but in the wake of the September 11 terrorist attacks on the World Trade Center and other important sites in America he condemned religious terrorism in all its ramifications. He declared, "I wish to reaffirm the Catholic Church's respect for Islam, for authentic Islam: the Islam that prays, that is concerned for others in need. Recalling the errors of the past, including the most recent past, all believers ought to unite their efforts to ensure that God is never made the hostage of human ambitions." The pontiff made it clear that fanaticism, terrorism and hatred are offensive to God and that to use them in the name of God is a profanation of that name.[122]

(ii) The Church's Relations with Hinduism, Buddhism, Traditional Religion

The Church has also great respect for all other genuine religious traditions and has made efforts to enter into dialogue of one kind or another with most of them. We shall now briefly see the relations of the Church with only three of them, namely, Hinduism, Buddhism, and the traditional religion.

The Second Vatican's *Nostra Aetate* treats all these religions under its second article. It observes that through-out the history of man, "there is found among different peoples a certain awareness of a hidden power, which lies behind the course of nature and the events of human life;" and that among some people, there is found "even the recognition of a supreme being, or still more of a father." The consequence of this awareness or recognition of a supernatural power is a way of life that is usually "imbued with a deep religious sense." The resultant religions, especially the more advanced of them, endeavor in different ways to answer man's existential questions. "Thus, in Hinduism men explore the divine mystery and express it both in limitless riches of myth and the accurately defined insights of philosophy." They seek deliverance from the trials of earthly life by a life of asceticism, meditation and confident reliance on or trust in God. Hinduism in its different forms bears testimony to "the essential inadequacy of this changing world", and lays out a way of life "by which men can, with confidence . . . , attain a state of perfect liberation and reach supreme illumination either through their own efforts or by the aid of divine help." And other non-Christian religions found all over the world endeavor in various ways to soothe men's hearts by offering a program of life that includes "doctrine, moral precepts and sacred rites."[123]

The Catholic Church respects all these and admonishes its members to enter "with prudence and charity" into dialogue with members of non-Christian religions; they should, "while witnessing to their own faith and way of life, acknowledge, preserve and encourage the moral truths found among non-Christians, also their social life and culture." The following are examples of the improvement of the relations between the Church and these religions since *Nostra Aetate* was published.

In India where Hinduism originated and where most Hindus live, the Indian Catholic church organizes in various parts of the country almost yearly inter-religious seminars. The organizers take cognizance of the fact that pilgrimages, meditation and prayer are part of the life of the people and therefore include them in their plan. In one such meeting, that of November 1980, the directors of the dialogue groups met in a meditation prayer session for four days in a Hindu pilgrimage center, the *ashram* of Rishikesh. The Hindus were overwhelmed with joy which was expressed on their behalf on the final day by a *swami*, the president of the *ashram* who said, "To the extent that you come out in openness, we Hindus will reach out to you in openness."[124]

During his visit to India early in 1986, Pope John Paul II on February 1 visited the Raj Ghats, the monument where are found the ashes of the body of Mahatma Gandhi, one of the most exemplary

Hindus that ever lived. Speaking here the pope referred to the resemblance of Gandhi's thoughts to the Beatitudes of Jesus Christ. He pointed out that the justice and the peace which are badly needed in today's society can be attained only by following the path which was the core of Gandhi's teaching: "the supremacy of the spirit and *Satyagrapha,* the 'truth force', which conquers without violence by the dynamism intrinsic to just action." The power of truth, he said, leads one as it led Gandhi, to recognize "the dignity, the equality, and fraternal solidarity of all human beings" and prompts one "to reject every form of discrimination." It shows rather the "need for mutual understanding, acceptance and collaboration between religious groups" in a pluralistic society.[125] Also in his address to non-Christian religious leaders, the pope quoting from various Hindu texts stressed the importance of dialogue, which he said makes possible collaboration in solving the world's problems.[126]

Progress in the relations of the Church with Hinayana (or the stricter denomination of) Buddhism varies in countries where this denomination of Buddhism is predominant, namely Burma, Cambodia, Laos, Thailand, and Sri Lanka. Progress is slow in Burma; the initial progress made in Cambodia and Laos has been cut short by the triumph of communism in these places. In Thailand, much progress has been made; the bishops' conference has an active commission for dialogue with Buddhists; inculturation is taken seriously. And during his visit to Thailand in 1984, Pope John Paul II commended the harmonious co-existence of Christians and Buddhists. In that visit, the pope made a courtesy visit to the supreme Buddhist patriarch.[127]

In Sri Lanka, where four great religions, namely, Buddhism, Hinduism, Islam, and Christianity, have co-existed for centuries, the bishops' conference organizes inter-religious encounters in many dioceses.[128]

There has been more progress in Mahayana (or popular) Buddhist countries, notably, Japan, Korea, and Taiwan. In Japan there are several organs that are helpful for dialogue between Christians and non-Christians at different levels. At the institutional level there is the bishops' commission for non-Christians; at the academic level there are several institutes of religion, culture and research; at the social level, the dominant bodies are the World Conference on Religion and Peace, and the Japan Religious Committee for the World Federation: at the experiential level are the Zen-Christian colloquium and the inter-monastic East-West exchange; and at the grassroots level there are the dialogue of life, inter-religious youth encounters and many pilgrimages from Japan to Rome.[129] Much progress has also being made in South Korea; there is a bishops' commission for ecumenism and inter-religious dialogue. The pope's address to non-Christian religious leaders in South Korea on May 6, 1984 is an evident sign of the Church's desire to enter into dialogue there with the predominant Buddhism and other religions. He said that the diversity in beliefs, both religious and ethical, makes it urgent for Christians and all believers "to foster genuine fraternal dialogue and to give special consideration to what human beings have in common and what promotes fellowship among them." Such concerted effort, he said, would create an atmosphere of peace "in which justice and compassion" can flourish.[130]

The Church's relations with the natural or traditional religion (the religion based on belief in God, in spirits, in ancestors and unclarified super-human beings and in the cult of these, best known in Africa south of the Sahara) have been mainly in the sphere of inculturation and adaptation to the culture of the people. Thanks to the progress made by ethnological and anthropological studies Christians have come to know more about this religion. Among the research centers, the Centre d'Etudes des Religieuses Africaines of the faculty of Catholic theology in Kinshasa ranks first.[131]

Challenges with Buddhism, Hinduism, and African Traditional Religion

Dialogue with Buddhism faces various challenges. Among them may be mentioned the fact that for Buddhists, especially in

Hinayana or strict Buddhist countries, such as Thailand and Sri Lanka, the national culture is identified with Buddhism, making it very difficult for Christians there to avoid syncretism. In addition, there are many divisions within Buddhism. In Japan, for instance, there are five main branches of Buddhism constituting one hundred and sixty denominations. In such a case it is not easy to find the official representatives of the religion.[132]

Dialogues with Hinduism and African traditional religion suffer also because it is not easy to find official representatives who can represent a wide geographical area of these religions. Furthermore, members of these religions have suspicions as to the motive of Christians for dialogue, and are sometimes unwilling to discuss their religion with Christians.[133] And lately, extremist Hindu groups in India have vowed to step up efforts to stop any conversions to Christianity in their country. This followed Pope John Paul II's visit to New Delhi, India to release the document *Ecclesia in Asia,* which, among other things, called for a new evangelization in Asia.[134]

Conclusion

In this chapter and the preceding ones we have considered the relations of the Catholic Church with different non-Christian religions. Though the relations between the Church and these religious traditions vary, the Church respects and shows good will to them and their good qualities. It is of the view that all sincere religions are different ways of searching for happiness which the human heart tirelessly longs for; that is, different ways of searching for the one divine reality, by whom and for whom man was created and to whom he must ultimately go. This became evident when Pope John Paul II invited all religions in the world to come together at Assisi and pray on October 27, 1986; each religion in turn praying in its own way in the presence of the others.[135] Speaking later to the Roman Curia about this event, the pope said that the fact that all these different religions were able to come together "to pray, fast and walk in silence" is "a clear sign of the profound unity of those who seek in religion spiritual and transcendent values that respond to the great questions of the human heart", despite their divisions.[136] As noted earlier in this book, this is one of the main theological bases for the Church's friendly attitude to or dialogue with non-Christian religions. The Church wishes to make these religions aware, through its dialogue with them, that all human beings have one common origin, God, and that all religions of the world are basically searching for this one God who is also the goal of all mankind. This, it is thought, will help many religions to seek harmonious collaborations rather than pitch camps against each other in cutthroat rivalry, opposition or oppression of one another. Pope John Paul II again, speaking to the plenary assembly of the Vatican Secretariat for Inter-religious Dialogue, summarizes much of what has been said about the basis, aims and manner of the Church's relations or dialogue with non-Christian religions. The pope reiterates that "dialogue is fundamental for the Church which is called to collaborate in God's plan with its method of presence, respect and love towards all persons." He makes it clear that dialogue is based on the very life of the triune God. This God, he notes, is the father or Lord of the one human family. "Christ has joined every person to himself" and the Spirit of God "works in each individual"; hence "dialogue is based on love for the human person as such who is the primary and fundamental way of the Church", the pope concludes.[137]

And on the twenty-fifth anniversary of the Assisi World Day of Prayer, that is, October 27, 2011 leaders of all world religions as well as leading agnostics gathered again at Assisi at the invitation of Pope Benedict XVI. Addressing them the pope noted that since the past twenty-five years some progress had been made in bridging the division of the world into opposing blocs as symbolized by the fall of the Berlin Wall three years after the meeting or pilgrimage at Assisi. He attributed the progress made thus far due partly to the prayers of the religions. He, however, lamented that despite the fact that there was no threat of imminent world war, the world was full of discord and violence. He identified two main types of violence.[138]

One was terrorism, often motivated by religious extremism. The pontiff regretted that instead of being an instrument for peace religion was sometimes used to create violence. He reiterated the position of the delegates of the Assisi conference of 1986 that violence is not part of religion. He challenged the delegates to find out what religions have in common and to identify the nature of true religion, urging all to undergo purification. He also pointed out the other great evil facing the world. That was secularism or the sense of the absence of God, his denial which leads to the loss of humanity. This had led to great cruelty and violence of alarming proportions, citing the Nazi concentration camps as examples of the evils of the denial of God could lead to. Thanks to secularism, he noted, some people worship money, power and material things sacrificing human dignity for personal gain while others seek happiness in material substance and leading to dependence on drugs. Summarizing, the pope states that the absence of God leads to the decline of man and humanity. Religions should discover God and point him out to others for world peace.[139]

We can see that it is evident that the Church today is seriously committed to friendly relations or dialogue with non-Christian religions. It is willing to express friendly gestures to all, "so that mutual understanding and collaboration may grow; so that moral values may be strengthened; so that God may be praised in all creation."[140]

CHAPTER FIVE

THE UNIVERSAL SIGNIFICANCE OF JESUS

So far we have been considering the Church's dialogue with non-Christian religions. In this chapter we shall concentrate on Jesus Christ, belief in whom or lack of it is the main difference between Christians and non-Christians. We shall endeavor to show why Christians believe in him and why he is seen as the absolute or universal savior. The aim of the chapter then is to help Christians, and especially those who engage in inter-religious dialogue, to have some clear idea of who and what Jesus is. This, it is supposed, will help them in their approaches and discussions. The chapter will therefore endeavor to vindicate the Christian claim: it will present the main reasons why Christians believe that Jesus is God and hence why he has universal salvific significance. But before we begin, it is important to bear in mind that we are not going to see a watertight demonstrable proof; for such a proof is rarely used in theology or in our dealings with God in general. However, the chapter will present enough reasons for belief in Jesus as God. Perhaps some Christians may consider presenting these reasons unnecessary. However, in such a case I beg their indulgence. Even if they do not see the need for this now, they will surely see it before the end of the book. Those who nevertheless think they do not need these reasons may skip this chapter and go to the next one. If, however, the reader chooses to read the chapter I would suggest that he do so with an open and unbiased mind.

1. The Eschatological Claim of Jesus

A careful reading of the Synoptic Gospels reveals that Jesus made an eschatological claim, a claim that he has a unique role in the coming of God's kingdom. According to these gospels, Jesus made this claim during his earthly ministry of healing, exorcism, and teaching which centered on the kingdom of God. But since Jesus in fact preached the kingdom of God and not himself, his statement about himself must be seen in the context of his proclamation of this kingdom which he claimed to usher in now for the first time.[141] Before considering this claim of Jesus it is helpful to have some background information about the origin and evolution of the notion of the kingdom of God before Jesus, that is, the notion in the Old Testament. This will enable us to appreciate the implication of Jesus' proclamation and claim within the context of this proclamation.

The Notion of the Kingdom of God in the Old Testament

The notion of the kingdom of God was not invented by either Jesus himself or his followers; it has deep roots in the Old Testament history and theology.[142] This notion underwent a non-systematic process of evolution during which it developed four main strands.

(a) *God's Saving Power in the History of His People.* God's reign over Israel was seen first and foremost in his saving work in the history of Israel. He delivered his people from slavery in Egypt, guided them through the desert, entered a covenant with them whereby he made a pledge to be their God in a special way; he gave them the Promised Land, protected them from their enemies, and brought them back from exile. In all these God was seen as a powerful king who brought these saving actions about by his saving power. The song of the Israelites after God saved them from the king of Egypt and his army through the Red Sea (Exodus chapter 15, especially verses 1-3, 17-18) is a good illustration of this. Israel's acknowledgement of God's saving power on its behalf and the allegiance it owes to him is the dominant motif of the Pentateuch or the first five books of the Bible; it is epitomized in the cultic creed of Deuteronomy 26: 5-10a.

(b) *God as Creator and Cosmic Ruler.* The second strand combines the acknowledgment of God's mighty deeds and his rule over the earth. It sees God as a mighty cosmic king who has all control over the universe and all the forces of nature. This is shown forcefully especially in the enthronement psalms. Examples are the following psalms: 93:1-2; 96:1, 10; 97:1-5: 98; 99; 47; 136.

(c) *The Experience of the Monarchy.* The major impulse to address God as king came with the establishment of the monarchy. The clan or tribal rule gave way to a more centralized and systematic government, the main aim of whose establishment was to protect the people from their war-like neighbors such as the Philistines. While God permitted the establishment of this institution, he himself was still seen as the real king over Israel. The human king was considered as endowed with divine authority and was expected to act in God's name and be submissive to him always.[143]

But the fears of Samuel and others who objected to the establishment of the monarchy[144] were justified when this institution seemed to be the main obstacle to proper conduct and Israel's true allegiance to God. The history of Israel's monarchy is a parade of failures, disappointments and compromises. Even David, considered as Israel's best king, exploited the poor and was guilty of adultery. The prophets' open condemnation of the injustices and failures of the monarchy together with the collapse of that institution itself paved the way for the post-exilic theology of the reign of God.

(d) *Eschatological Hope for God's Reign.* The eschatological hope for God's reign or salvation began during the exile and continued to grow in the post-exile period. The destruction of the Northern Kingdom and the exile of the South were seen by the prophets as punishment for the sins of Israel. Likewise their liberation by King Cyrus of Persia was considered as a sign of God's forgiveness. Cyrus was seen as an instrument of God, the real liberator.[145] Yet Israel still longed for total and final liberation, a period when it would be freed from the foreign rule under which it was subjected from time to time. At this time Israel's notion of God's reign or kingdom began to take on eschatological tones. Its monarchy was a complete failure and brought a lot of woes; and it was now and again subjected to foreign, pagan and often oppressive rulers, such as Antiochus Epiphanes who looted Israel's treasures and set up the "abomination of desolation," that is, the image of a pagan god, Zeus, within the temple sanctuary or Holy of Holies.[146] Israel was now in a serious dilemma. If given the option, would it choose to continue under foreign rule or to be liberated and have a monarchy similar to the one it had in the past? It would choose neither. But it did not lose hope. Looking back into their history and remembering God's saving deeds on their behalf in the past, his faithfulness to the covenant and promise of eternal dynasty to David (2 Sam. 7:11-13), which was renewed through the prophet Jeremiah (Jer. 23:5-6), the Israelites felt convinced that after all their sufferings God himself would establish his reign or kingdom over them. This kingdom would never be destroyed or pass to any other nation. [147]

Jesus and the Kingdom of God

Thus was set the stage when Jesus appeared on the scene. He claimed he was bringing about the coming of the long-awaited kingdom of God. Jesus proclaimed the closeness of the kingdom, the closeness of God; it is being ushered in now. The eschatological hope is being fulfilled in his time, Jesus claimed. "The time has come . . . and the kingdom of God is close at hand", he proclaimed (Mk. 1:14-15). Hence he counted as blessed those who saw his work and heard him: "Happy are the eyes that see what you see, for I tell you that many prophets and kings wanted to see what you see and never saw it; to hear what you hear and never heard it" (Lk. 10:23-24). And in his first public speech or sermon in his hometown Nazareth Jesus, after reading the lesson from the prophet, told his audience that the prophecy was fulfilled in him (Lk. 4:21): the time referred to by the promise of the prophets (that is, the time God would come in person to save his people) had arrived. As evidence of it, "The blind see again, the lame walk, lepers are cleansed, and the deaf hear, and the dead are raised to life and the good news is proclaimed to the poor" (Mt. 11:5). This is a direct reference to Isaiah[148] where these phenomena are given as signs of God's coming to save his people.[149]

But why did Jesus make these statements: why did he think he was now playing God's role? The answer to this question is important for us in this discussion. We endorse the position of most reputable contemporary theologians and biblical scholars who hold that Jesus thought in this way because he experienced a uniquely intimate relationship with God the Father, a relationship of sonship which no other person has, but which is significant for all since in it God's closeness to all mankind is inaugurated in a new and unsurpassable way. In this unique relationship with God the Father, Jesus was conscious that the coming of the kingdom of God was inseparably rooted in his person; hence he was conscious too that it was he who would have to usher it in by his life and proclamation. [150] This experience of unique intimacy with God explains too why Jesus called God "Abba", that is, "Dad" or "Daddy." It explains also why his method of teaching and acting differed from those of his predecessors and contemporary teachers. A cursory look would see Jesus as a rabbi or a teacher of wisdom or even as an ordinary prophet. But a careful observation discloses a real distinction between him and each of these groups. His contemporaries who noticed the difference, in their amazement exclaimed. "What is this? A new teaching and one proclaimed with authority" (Mk. 1:27). His method of teaching differs from that of the scribes or rabbis who simply explain the Law of Moses. Jesus, however, goes beyond the Bounds of the Law and thereby exceeds the bounds of Judaism. He places his word above the word or authority of Moses, the highest authority in Judaism. By his "but I say to you", Jesus makes a claim to say the last word on behalf of God or rather to be God's final word, bringing the word of God in the Old Testament to completion or fulfillment.[151]

His manner of speaking also differs from that of a prophet. It is the function of prophets to transmit the word of God, and those of the Old Testament made it clear that they were only transmitting God's word. Hence they said, "Thus says the Lord", "A saying of Yahweh", or similar introductory words or phrases. Unlike them Jesus spoke with his own authority (Mk.1:22; 2:10 ff) and never used such words. He makes no distinction between his own word and God's. Thus his unique and incomparable intimacy with God and his consciousness of this relationship set his person and proclamation higher than any prophet's. And unlike prophets too, Jesus alone claims the awareness that he will not be succeeded by another prophet who would speak a new and different word of God (cf. Mt.5-7; 24:35). Why? Because he was conscious of being the final word of God, after whom no other prophet can follow. This means that Jesus was conscious of being, or rather claimed to be the final or last word of God to which nothing more can be added. In other words, Jesus was conscious that in him God has said all that needs to be said; that in him God has spoken the last word.[152]

It is important to remember, however, that Jesus made his claim not only by words or preaching but also by his actions. Many exegetes today agree that there are firm historical bases to affirm that Jesus did in fact act as healer and exorcist. His actions made concrete the "good news", and the arrival here on earth of the kingdom of God which he proclaimed becomes revealed through the victory over evil or the powers of evil. He makes it clear that in the struggle against evil he is on the side of God; no one can be on both sides: "He who is not with me is against me" (Mk. 3:27). While some of his contemporaries accepted his saving acts of healing and exorcism as signs of God's closeness, his adversaries viewed them as backed by demonic powers (Mk. 3:22-30).[153]

Included in the claim made by action is Jesus' gathering of his disciples and his call for a decision. His manner of gathering disciples was different from that of the Jewish rabbis. His disciples did not choose him or request to follow him; he chose them and he did that without any pressure. He chose "those he wanted" (Mk. 3:33). As is evident from the Synoptic Gospels his call was not a request; it was not an invitation, nor was it a question nor an inducement or an offer: it was a command. In each case, as we see in the Synoptics, he saw these men while they were busy with their daily work and his summons was given, "Come, follow me" (Mk. 1:17; 1:20; 2:14). On each occasion they left their work and followed him immediately. His calls were urgent and demanded immediate and unconditional response. There was no place for anyone who procrastinated or postponed. And those called, again, were not called like the disciples of the scribes or Pharisees to participate in or conduct intellectual or learned disputations, but rather to share in the proclamation of the kingdom of God. This means sharing in his prerogative of announcing with authority the coming of God's kingdom and making this authority evident by driving away evil spirits (Mk.3:14; 6: 7). Furthermore, the relationship between Jesus and his disciples is not temporary; it lasts for ever. Jesus made it clear that his followers are disciples for ever, not teachers, for there is only one teacher (Mt. 10:24-25; 23:8). His call was also a call to a commitment to share his dangerous fate for better or for worse. Accepting such a call also demands breaking of ties; it demands leaving everything behind, risking everything and denying of oneself (Lk. 9:23-25; 14:26-27).

Similarly Jesus called people to a final decision, and linked the decision to accept or reject the kingdom of God specifically to the decision for or against him, his work or his word. This is evident in Mark 8:38-9:1. Thus Jesus claims that in relation to himself we make our choice about God. Making such a claim implies or is equivalent to claiming to be at least a unique envoy of God.[154]

In addition, we have to consider Jesus' eating with sinners and tax-collectors and his association with those considered ritually unclean. He was called the friend of sinners and tax-collectors (Mt. 11:9). The meaning of this behavior of Jesus has to be seen in connection with his message of the coming kingdom of God, the kingdom of love. His meals with this group were a sign of God's invitation to all to the eschatological banquet in his kingdom. There is an additional reason for this. Pious Jews at the time of Jesus did not associate with those considered to be morally or ritually unclean, much less eat with them until they were purified. Jesus, who was considered a pious Jew, by eating with sinners implicitly claimed to have purified them, that is, to have forgiven their sins. He was acting out what he verbalized thus: "Your sins are forgiven" (Mk.2:5). His contemporaries felt the seriousness of the claim and retorted. "He is blaspheming. Who can forgive sins but God?" (Mk. 2:7)[155]

Finally, Jesus accepted his death freely as something necessary in his mission; he considered it as the death of a prophet. For him it was a sacrificial death for the redemption of the world; a death that would in some way bring about the arrival of the kingdom of God. He maintained his claim even in dying. He, however, trusted that his triumph over death would vindicate his claim: it would show that his death is acceptable to God.[156]

In summary, Jesus in his message, person and action claimed to be God's final word. He claimed a unique intimacy with God which gave him the power to act for God in a way no other person could, to speak for God, call to conversion, forgive sins and perform other actions that were and still are considered as the prerogatives of God.

2. Validation of Jesus' Claim: The Resurrection

What has been said in this chapter so far is that Jesus claimed he had a unique role in the coming of the kingdom of God or rather to be the word of God, God's final word, or what traditional Christianity calls the Son of God. This claim can be validated not by considering the individual miracles he performed but rather by concentrating on the one in which his power was most manifest, his greatest miracle; that is, his resurrection.[157]

Information Helpful for Understanding the Resurrection of Jesus

(i) The Unity of the Death and Resurrection of Jesus

The death and resurrection of Jesus constitute a single unit despite the temporal interval between them. His death was the beginning of his glorification which culminated in his resurrection; it was a death oriented toward his resurrection.[158] Jesus was aware of this. That is why all his predictions about his death as related in the Synoptic Gospels are linked to his resurrection. It is because of this unity that the soteriological value of Christ's salvific work cannot be placed on either his death or his resurrection separately or independently of the other: his salvific work was accomplished through his death and resurrection. Sometimes his death and resurrection are mentioned together; at other times one of them alone (usually his death) is mentioned. In the second case, the unmentioned term of the pair is implied.[159] This is the way the terms are going to be used later in this book.

(ii) The Meaning of Resurrection

Some people wrongly understand resurrection as raising back to mortal life. The resurrection of Jesus and resurrection in general, however, does not mean the resuscitation of a corpse or reanimation of a dead material body or in common language the raising back to mortal life as, for instance, the raising of Lazarus or of Jairus's daughter. Lazarus or any other person simply raised from the dead was raised back to temporal life. Resurrection is not returning to our present existence of space and time or a continuation of earthly life as we know it. Those raised back to the life of space and time die again but a person who undergoes resurrection cannot die again; death has no more power over him (cf. Lk.20:35-36; Rom.6:9). One who undergoes resurrection rises to a new life, eternity. Resurrection therefore is the ultimate and definitive salvation of a human existence by God, the real validity or value of human life which endures for ever.[160] With regard to salvation resurrection cannot be seen in a neutral or indifferent manner; nor can it be negative. Resurrection has to be understood as the transformation of the material world or life of space and time into everlasting life free from suffering but full of joy. It is the very salvation of a human existence and the acceptance of that existence by God, the ultimate salvation which we who are still living the mortal life can know only in hope.[161] With this understanding, then, the resurrection of Jesus, if it is a fact, will mean the acceptance of his existence and cause by God; it will mean the permanent survival of his person and cause, that is, his claim to say the final word on behalf of God or to have a unique role in the coming of God's kingdom.

(iii) Our Transcendental Hope in Resurrection

Indispensable for understanding the resurrection of Jesus is our hope in our own resurrection. It is a truism to state that we all know we shall die, that our temporal existence will one day come to an end. We also know that this temporal end is not the end of the entire person. The human existence is more than a merely biological-psychic existence; the human person transcends matter. And that substance in man or the human person which transcends matter transcends also man's existence in space and time. This transcendent substance, however, should not be understood as only a part of the human person; it must be understood rather as the final and definitive substance of the human person. If a person therefore sees his life as meaningful, if he has the hope that his existence goes beyond temporal life, he is affirming his hope in his resurrection or eternity; and eternity here, again, is not an endless continuation of time but rather the ultimate and definitive value of the human person's existence which has been brought to a successful end and fulfilled in freedom. Anyone who has made a morally good decision in a matter of life and death so that nothing accrues to him except the presumed good has experienced something of eternity. In other words, anyone who has made a personal sacrifice for a morally good action or cause without a hope of selfish or material gain has some experience of what eternity means.[162] There are two instances which can illustrate this point. One of them is Mahatma Gandhi's case. In a bloody religious civil war resulting in the partition of India into Hindu India and Moslem Pakistan, Moslems and Hindus were killing each other in a very bloody civil war. Every effort to bring about the cessation of hostilities failed. Gandhi, himself a Hindu, started to fast and vowed not to eat until the killings would stop, even if it meant his fasting to death. Eventually the war ended thanks to his fast and mediation.[163]

Another example is the case of St. Maximilian Kolbe. During the Second World War, in reprisal for one prisoner's escape, Nazi officers chose ten other prisoners to die. One of these was a young husband and father who grieved excessively for his everlasting separation from his young family. Father Maximilian Kolbe sympathized with him and offered himself in exchange for this young man.[164] Most people at one time or another have some experience of something of eternity. For instance, the strong desire for fulfillment or happiness, a desire which is hardly satisfied by anything in this life, is an indication of existence after temporal life. This forms part of man's hope for future survival or rather man's transcendental hope in resurrection. And this transcendental hope in resurrection is the only context within which we can experience something of or understand the resurrection of Jesus. This means that if we have transcendental hope in our own resurrection or have experienced something like it, as in the case of Gandhi or Maximilian Kolbe, then we can understand or believe the reality of the resurrection of Jesus.[165]

The Resurrection of Jesus as a Unique Fact

There are grounds for faith in the resurrection of Jesus as a unique fact. To begin with, we challenge anyone who considers such faith an error to explain why this type of error (that is, an assertion of or belief in other cases of resurrection) does not occur more frequently.[166] According to the New Testament, shortly after Jesus' crucifixion and burial, his followers began to proclaim that he had risen from the dead and was to be acknowledged as the Messiah or the Christ (Phil. 2:9-11; Rom.1:3-4). The story of the resurrection of Jesus could not be an invention of his followers. For according to Jewish belief a person crucified was thought to be cursed by God; and a crucified and resurrected Messiah was unthinkable and absurd.[167] Yet the first Christians (the apostolic witness) insist that the crucified Jesus is risen and is Messiah. Faith in his resurrection is dependent on this apostolic witness that is, on the witness of those who had the first experience of the risen Jesus, an experience that was quite unique, different from all religious experiences including even mystical visions and cannot be duplicated. We accept the apostolic witness not only because the witnesses were obviously unselfish and honest people but also and especially because the transcendental hope in resurrection which we have makes it possible for us to receive such testimony as insiders, as people who have some experience of what Jesus has achieved fully. There is here mutual inter-dependence or inter-reinforcement between our transcendental hope in resurrection and the faith in the apostolic witness. On the one hand, if our transcendental hope is not denied it naturally seeks its categorical confirmation in some concrete historical event in which it can become explicit. It finds such an event in the resurrection of Jesus thanks to the apostolic witness. And on the other hand, we accept the apostolic witness without great difficulty, owing to our transcendental hope. Furthermore, the apostolic witness is supported by our experience of the Spirit of the risen Jesus who bears witness to us that he is alive.[168]

In addition to what has already been said, we have to recall that according to the New Testament, by his resurrection, Jesus was made "Lord" and "Messiah" (Acts 2:36). Even though he was both of this right from the beginning of his human existence, these titles attained their historical climax and tangibility for us in his resurrection. His resurrection is also his exaltation and enthronement as judge and Lord over all creation. And by this enthronement Jesus has begun the life of the kingdom he proclaimed. This means his sharing in God's power and accounts for the radical transformation in his followers or disciples. Those men, who in fear abandoned their master during his suffering, were able to come out shortly after his death and proclaim his message openly and fearlessly, even accusing to their very face the authorities responsible for his death. What explanation can be given for this unusual change? The apostolic witness says that this was brought about by the Spirit of the risen Jesus in whom his followers now see God.[169]

The testimony of the apostolic witness includes the appearances of the risen Jesus (1 Cor. 15:5-8; Lk 24.34, Mk.16.7, Acts 10.40f, 13:30f; Jn. 20:11-18); the activities of his Spirit (Acts 2:1ff; 5:7ff; 13 :2; 16:7; 18:9); and the empty tomb. Even though from what we have learned so far about the meaning of resurrection the empty tomb by itself alone cannot prove the resurrection of Jesus, it, however, adds weight to other testimonies. Not even the early opponents of Christianity could deny that the tomb of Jesus was empty. Rather than deny it they alleged that his body had been stolen (Mt. 28:11-15). In addition, the attribution of the discovery of the empty tomb to women adds even greater weight to the reliability of the story. For if the story of the resurrection of Jesus was a legend made up by the early Christians they would have attributed the discovery to men rather than to women, whose witness in the contemporary Jewish culture was not accepted as valid.[170]

From what we have seen so far we can say that the resurrection of Jesus is credible; it is a unique fact. Therefore his eschatological claim, that is, the claim that he has a unique role in the coming of God's kingdom, the claim to say the final word on behalf of

God or rather to be God's final word is vindicated. He is the final prophet, taking *prophet* here to mean one who speaks for God on a concrete situation and calls people to a decision. He is the prophet who claims his word is final and absolute. This is a claim no other genuine prophet can make. Thus with the claim of his word Jesus is a prophet who surpasses all others and in whom the essence of a prophet is epitomized. He indeed is the final word of God. By saying Jesus is the final word of God we mean here that in Jesus God has said all that he has to say: there is nothing more to say because he has offered his very self in Jesus. [171] In other words, Jesus is the very self-expression of God; he is the very revelation of God; as the New Testament puts it, "He is the image of the unseen God" (Col. 1:15), "the perfect copy of his nature" (Heb. 1:3). For in him "God is most fully disclosed to us, discovered by us, made accessible to us."[172] In Jesus we meet "God and his glory . . . . He is God's kingdom, God's word and God's love in person."[173] To say therefore that Jesus is the word of God is to say, in other words, that he is the Son of God—as traditional Christianity puts it: that is to say, he is of the same substance as God: he is God.

It may be good to ask here if Jesus' resurrection is of any value to the believer. In ordinary language Jesus resurrection means that the gate of heaven that was closed by sin was opened by Jesus through his death and resurrection. At his resurrection he opened wide the gate of paradise and made it possible for us to go to heaven. Without his resurrection there would be no hope of heaven: we now have hope of going to heaven because he by his resurrection has gone there before us and expects us to be with him there. By his resurrection he initiates the process of our own resurrection or salvation. (For our resurrection is another name for our salvation.) That is why Christians rejoice and celebrate Easter with joy. He now takes his seat at the right hand of the Father to welcome his followers into his heavenly home. This is in fulfillment of his promise. We remember he said, "In my Father's house there are many dwelling places . . . I am going to prepare a place for you. And if I go and prepare a place for you, I will come back again and take you to myself, so that where I am you also may be."[174]

Now, from the knowledge we have gained about Jesus we can have a new and higher knowledge of the meaning of man or the human person. If the man Jesus, as man, is the self-utterance or very self-expression of God, if God has become man in Jesus, then man is that which happens when God empties himself outside of himself. We shall see more on this in the next chapter.

The very fact that God has assumed our nature in the man Jesus renders human nature and human history henceforth irrevocably redeemed and says what man is: the emptiness into which God could empty himself. Jesus, the God-man, is God's explanation of what man is. It is in the mystery of the God-man, the mystery of the Word made flesh that the mystery or nature of man becomes clear. His incarnation, as it were, bridged the chasm between God and man, so that God is now man and remains man for ever. In Jesus, the God man, as we have seen above, God's historical offer of himself to mankind is manifest; he is the very self-expression of God. As man, his death, which resumes his life of total surrender to God, represents mankind's response or acceptance of God's offer. And his resurrection or triumph over death is a clear vindication of his acceptance by God on behalf of mankind. He is the personification of God's reaching out to mankind and mankind's response to God's offer. He is our perfect "yes" to God, the exemplar of the creature's surrender to the creator. He is the bridge between God and man. Through him alone can anybody participate in the mystery of God, in God's self-communication in grace in this life or in the beatific vision hereafter.[175] He is the only mediator between God and man (1Tim. 2:5), the only way to God and salvation (Jon. 14:6); he is the absolute or universal savior of mankind.

The idea of Jesus being the universal savior of mankind takes nothing away from God's universal salvific will: the two rather work hand in hand. God's salvific will establishes the life of Jesus which reaches its fulfillment in death, a death which in turn makes God's universal salvific will manifest and irrevocable. Therefore the life and death of Jesus taken together are the *cause* of God's universal salvific will in the sense of quasi-sacramental and real symbolic causality: the universal salvific will of God inaugurates itself really and irreversibly in the life and death of Jesus. In other words, the death of Jesus (which resumes his life of total surrender) along with his resurrection, posited as a sacramental sign, causes historically and irrevocably what is signified, God's salvific will.[176] Hence it is rightly said that Jesus is the sacrament of God. To put it simply, God wishes and plans salvation to come to mankind through Jesus Christ and through him alone. Hence the Christian tradition teaches that there is no salvation except through him (Acts 4:12); no one can be saved except through Jesus. In the next chapter we shall revisit some of the main ideas here.

CHAPTER SIX

THE UNIQUENESS OF THE CHURCH AS A WAY OF SALVATION

The Church as Sacrament

In the chapter immediately preceding this we noted that Jesus is the sacrament of God. We know that a sacrament is an external sign of invisible grace which contains or produces the grace it signifies.[177] As the sacrament of God, Jesus contains the grace he signifies, and conversely, he signifies and confers or gives the grace he contains. In Jesus the inward or invisible grace of God becomes visible or sensible. The sacrament of redemption, however, is not complete in Jesus as an individual. In order to become the sign that he ought to be, he has to appear as the sign of God's redeeming love extending toward the whole human race, and of the response of the whole of humanity to that redeeming love. This appearance he makes in the form of his redeeming community, the Church. The Church is therefore primarily a sign or rather sacrament. If Jesus is the sacrament of God, the Church in turn is the sacrament of Jesus.[178]

To make clearer this point we have to employ here the concept of *symbol* whose meaning modern phenomenology and theology have very much enriched. In theology today *symbol* does not mean simply an indicative sign or a mere projection of the unconscious, akin to dreams: it is more than that. A symbol is rather a sign charged with much meaning and even emotion. There are two main types of symbol, the representative symbol and the real symbol. The representative symbol refers the mind to something unreal or absent, as for instance the photograph of a friend some four thousand miles away. The real symbol on the other hand exists simultaneously with and makes present what it signifies. The human body, for instance, is the real symbol of the human interior, the human spirit. For the body, by its actions, makes present here and now what is in the human spirit, the interior.[179] Another name for real symbol may be sacrament. We shall use the two terms interchangeably in this chapter. Now, after his resurrection (which is more than physical rising as we noted above), Jesus, who is totally penetrated by the Spirit, sent this Spirit, *his* Spirit upon his followers, his saving community, the Church.[180] Hence he is present in his Church in the Holy Spirit. Thus the Church is the continuation of the historical presence of Christ the missionary. Just as the human body is the real symbol of the human spirit so also is the Church the real symbol or sacrament of Christ because Jesus is present in it in his Spirit. This is why it is sometimes also called the mystical body of Christ. It is on this fact (the fact that the Church is the continued historical presence or mystical body of Christ) that credibility in the sacraments and other liturgical practices of the Church have their basis, and without it the whole sacramental system of the Church would be pure magic. The Second Vatican Council stresses the presence of Christ in the Church.[181] This presence is often taken for granted especially in the celebration of the Eucharist. The Church would not be able to celebrate a valid Eucharist if it were not the historical continuation of Christ's presence in the world. It is "the historical tangibility of the salvific will of God as revealed in Christ."[182] Hence the Second Vatican Council calls it in relation to Christ, a "sacrament—a sign and instrument, that is, of communion with God."[183] It is through this sacrament, the Church, then, that Jesus, the savior of the world, usually makes available the salvation he has won for the human race. This is to say that the Church is the ordinary way of salvation, the salvation which Christ won for mankind.

From the Point of View of Salvation History

We have considered this subject from the point of view of sacrament. Let us also consider it from the point of view of salvation history. Perhaps, it will appear clearer from this viewpoint, since there will be more facts to support our position. We shall begin with the notion of covenant in the Bible.

Notion of Covenant

In the Bible, especially in the Old Testament, making of covenants was common among the people. A covenant, unlike a simple contract, was usually a solemn ritual agreement by which each of the parties involved solemnly bound itself to be totally committed to the welfare of the other party just as it was committed to its own welfare. In other words, by a covenant the parties, as it were, exchanged not only their interests but also their persons. This was why covenants were used in marriage agreements. They were also used in other serious agreements or pacts. If the words of a typical biblical covenant could be summed up, they could be stated thus: "I am yours, you are mine; my life for your life." Usually after such a covenant a very close bond similar to the family bond was created between the covenanted parties. For instance, if the family of Chidi entered a covenant with the family of Chima, Chidi could be treated as a member of the family of Chima and vice versa. Chima could call the members of Chidi's family "my people." And other people could rightly call the members of Chidi's family "Chima's people." Thus typical covenants created families or communities similar to families. There were ritual blessings for the keeping of the covenant and imprecations for its violation. The seriousness of a covenant is indicated by the fact that it was ratified (signed) or sealed with blood. The blood not only represented the creating of a blood relationship or bond between the parties but was also a reminder to each of them that the first to break the terms of the covenant would undergo the fate of the victim whose blood was used in the covenant. That is to say, that party should die or suffer the imprecations invoked in the covenant. The same curses or blessings redound on the parties who later renew a covenant, even if they were not present when the covenant was originally made.[184] Let us keep these ideas in mind as we go on.

In the book of Genesis God made a covenant with Noah after the flood. Later, he made another covenant with Abraham. Abraham became the ancestor of the twelve tribes of Israel. This covenant was the basis of God's relationship with the Hebrews.

At Sinai, after the Israelites had been freed from slavery, God demanded that they enter into a covenant with him. By this covenant God makes clear his choice of a people, the nation of Israel, as his special people. The people become God's special possession, a holy nation, a kingdom of priests. This implies that Israel will act as mediator between God and other peoples. Although he is the God of the whole universe, he will be the God of Israel in a special way. As long as the Israelites are faithful to the covenant, God will protect them from every danger. The nation on its part must keep the terms of the covenant; it must be faithful to the Law (Ex. 19:5; 24:7-8). The nation receives the Law, the Ten Commandments and the book of the covenant (i.e. Ex. 20:22-23:33). The Law witnesses against the nation; its transgression cancels the promises and invites the anger of God. Moses splashes the blood of the covenant on the altar representing God and on the people reminding the people that it is the blood of the covenant (Ex, 24:3-8). This is to show the establishment of a union of life between the parties. This covenant is elsewhere summed up in the formula "You shall be my people and I will be your God" (Jer. 7:23; 11:4; 24:7; Ezk. 11:20; 14:11; Hos. 2:25). It was this covenant that constituted the Israelites into a people, the People of God. It imposed on them the duty of worshipping the Lord God and no other god.

But Israelites soon failed to keep the terms of the covenant. Many times they worshipped false gods or mixed the worship of God with the worship of alien gods. Thus they started to live and behave like the people around them, failing to trust in God alone but sometimes relied on the same source of protection or power as their enemies. From the eighth century B. C. on the prophets pointed out to them the consequences of their behavior: it would bring God's judgment; but if they repented and came back to the covenant, they would receive God's pardon and grace. Despite these warnings of the prophets and the reforms of King Josiah, the Israelites remained essentially disloyal to the covenant and to God. It was during this period that these prophets foretold a new covenant that God would make with his people. This economy would surpass the plan of Sinai. By it, God would give his special gift to each one and would make possible the knowledge of God's will and the power to follow that will (Jer. 31:31-34; Ezk. 36: 25-28; Hos. 2: 20f.). It is against this background that we shall consider the new covenant made by Jesus on behalf of the new People of God, a people that emerged from this new covenant.

The New People of God

Jesus, the Son of God, came to preach the message of salvation to the entire people of Israel and the world. The first phase of his plan was to help the Israelites to renew their covenant relationship with God so that they might be of some help in God's plan to bring the whole human race back to God through Christ. That was why he limited his public ministry and that of his original disciples to the house of Israel (Mt. 10:5-6; 15:24). But most of the Israelites rejected him and his message. When this was the case, while not rejecting the Jewish people, who were the old People of God, Jesus embarked on his larger plan or rather God's plan of founding a new saving community or new People of God, the Church.

Jesus knew himself to be commissioned by the Father to save his people. Through him God's promises to the patriarchs, which are irrevocable (Rom. 9:6), would be carried out. The carrying out of these promises through history to their ultimate goal of salvation would, however, be effected through a new people. This new people, a new community of salvation made up of Jews and Gentiles, had to take over the historical mission of Israel, the mission to be the community of salvation for the human race. Obligated to walk in the faith of Abraham, this new community becomes the new posterity, the true seed of Abraham, that inherits the promises made to the patriarch (Rom. 4:12-16; 9:6-8; Gal. 4:28). But God's covenant with the new people does not imply the annulment of the old covenant but rather its continuation and fulfillment. However, in the days to come salvation would not be fixed or tied to a national identity (Mt, 8:1 ff. Lk. 13:28f). The dividing line should no longer be between the circumcised and the uncircumcised but rather between those who are baptized in the name of Jesus Christ and walk in his ways and those who are not. Those thus baptized, both Jews and Gentiles, form the new People of God (Rom. 9). It is they who constitute the Church.

The Founding of the Church

Our discussion on the founding of the Church will bring to light the importance Jesus attaches to this institution and the role he wants it to play in the salvation of the human race.

Before his death Jesus made preparations for the Church. Early in his public ministry he chose the Twelve. But the most important of his acts of preparation was the institution of a communal meal for his new community. He instituted this at his last meal with the Twelve and within the context of the Jewish Passover. Also of great importance are Christ's promise to and commissioning of Peter. Even though the whole life of Jesus was oriented toward founding the Church, these two acts are of unique importance. We shall now see how Jesus carried out his or rather God's plan to found the Church.

76

(i) The Institution of the Eucharist.

According to the New Testament narration of the institution of the Eucharist (Mt.26:26-29; Mk.14:22-26; Lk. 22:14-20; 1 Cor. 11:24-25), Jesus combines in his person the roles of the paschal lamb, the *ebed Yahweh* or Servant of the Lord of Deutero-Isaiah, and the victim of the covenant. The paschal lamb was the victim whose blood saved the first-born sons of Israelites just before their exodus from Egypt (Ex. 12). In Deutero-Isaiah is found the Servant of the Lord, a mysterious and innocent personage who through his vicarious representation and suffering becomes the ransom for many (Is. 53:4-12). Through his atoning death which is anticipated and symbolized in this meal, Jesus, like the paschal lamb and the Servant of the Lord, will be the ransom for the salvation of many. All four accounts include Jesus' indication that his body or his blood is given for the salvation of "many" or "you" which is reminiscent of the role of the paschal lamb and even more of the Servant of the Lord (Is. 53:11-12). And as the victim of the covenant, his blood ratifies or seals the covenant that establishes the family relationship between God and a new people, thus forming the new People of God.

On the evening before his death, Jesus had with the Twelve, the inner circle of his disciples, a paschal or Passover dinner, the Jewish ritual meal which commemorates the exodus from Egypt and the constitution of Israelites into a people, the People of God. According to the Synoptic Gospels, at this dinner, Jesus expresses his delight at having that epochal meal with his disciples. He assures them that he will not eat of that meal again until it is fulfilled in "the kingdom of God" (Lk. 22:18). What does he mean by this? The meaning of Jesus' intention here can only be understood in the light of his imminent death and resurrection. Here he means that as far as he (and the new people he is about to establish) is concerned that meal is the last Passover meal of the old covenant and the beginning of a new one. His imminent death and resurrection will mark the end of the old era and the beginning of the new one: by his anticipated death and resurrection he will effect a new covenant that will supersede the Sinaitic covenant and usher in the kingdom of God.

All four accounts agree that Jesus has in mind the making of a covenant, for all have it that Jesus gave his disciples the cup as the blood of the covenant (Mt. 26:28; Mk. 14:24; Lk. 22:20; 1 Cor. 11:25). Luke and Paul make it clear that it is specifically the new covenant long foretold by the prophets, as indicated above, for both in their accounts have, "For this cup is the new covenant in my blood." Thus according to the New Testament accounts, through this communal ritual meal, which is the symbolic action[185] of his death together with the anticipated death and resurrection, Jesus effected the new covenant between God and his new people, thereby creating a new community, a saving community, the new People of God. Here lies the high point of Christ's redemptive work. While it is true that his salvific work includes atonement for sins, the greatest benefit we gain from this work is the fact that we are introduced into and made members of God's family thanks to the new covenant. The salvation Christ won for us, in other words, is not simply the forgiveness of sins. While it does not exclude this, it is something far more than that: we are made sons and daughters of God through the new covenant ratified or sealed with Christ's blood. Just as the old covenant, sealed with blood, made the Israelites the old People of God, even more so the new covenant, sealed with the blood of Christ, makes the new Israelites (Christ's followers) the new People of God, or new family of God. Here too is to be underscored the importance of the Eucharist in building up the Church, the new People of God. The foundation and growth of the Church owe much to its institution and celebration, for it is the sacrament of the covenant by which the Church, as the new saving family of God, was created. Its celebration is the renewal, or rather, re-enactment of that covenant and continues to build up the Church and its members. (Hence the saying, "The Church makes the Eucharist and the Eucharist makes the Church.")

This meal that Jesus takes with his disciples is also the new Passover meal. The Jewish Passover commemorates the saving of

78

Israel from slavery and its constitution into a people, the People of God, through the Sinaitic covenant.[186] The new meal (which is the sacrament of Christ's redeeming death and resurrection) will now commemorate not the saving events of Egypt or Sinai but rather Jesus' saving event and the constitution of the new saving community. Therefore Jesus now gives his followers the command to celebrate henceforth this new ritual meal in place of the Jewish Passover meal. By this command he ordained his apostles priests and hereby instituted the Christian priesthood which ensures the celebration of the new Passover until he comes in glory. Henceforth when his followers take part in the Passover celebration it is not the Jewish Passover that they will celebrate but the Christian Passover, the Passover of Christ and the new people he has won for God. That is the meaning of his words, "do this in memory of me" or "in remembrance of me" (Lk. 22:19; 1 Cor. 11:24, 25). (But we should also not forget that "in memory of me" or "in remembrance of me" here is not simply calling to mind Jesus' saving work. It means also "reenact my saving work when you do this") The Eucharist is a "memorial" then in the sense that it is a cultic reenactment of the saving event of Calvary; by it the participant experiences the saving event and is personally integrated into the death and resurrection of Jesus Christ. This happens when a person properly and fully participates in the celebration of the Mass.[187] Worthy of note are Jesus' words: "Take and eat, this is my body . . . ; take and drink is my blood." He means here that he gives himself unconditionally to his followers in an unprecedented manner. By the new covenant, he and his followers have become, as it were, blood relations. He becomes united with them and they also spiritually become united with one another in such an intimate manner that it is difficult to explain. Paul attempts to explain this in one of his letters (see 1Cor. 10:16-17). By offering the bread and wine as the real representations or rather sacrament of his body which is to be broken and his blood which will be poured away or shed, Jesus means that he surrenders himself totally and unconditionally to the Father for the welfare of the human race. At the same time he gives himself unconditionally to the human race itself.[188] It may be useful to note that those who were present at the institution of the Eucharist participated in this meal. Just as the participants in the Passover meal in Egypt partook of the paschal Lamb in order to be saved from the anticipated death so also those who eat of the new Passover Lamb will be saved from eternal death. The new Passover Lamb is consumed sacramentally under the appearance of bread and wine. And those who thus partake of it properly are promised integration into Christ and eternal life (Jn. 6:51-58). Christ desires to give himself continually in an ever sanctifying manner. Those who participate in his new Passover or the Mass are sanctified by him, if they receive him well.

Here without minding running into the risk of repetition, I wish to stress once more the importance of the Eucharist in the founding of the Church. Jesus instituted the Eucharist as the sacrament of the sacrifice of the new covenant which he effected between God and the new People of God. He did this in the context of the Jewish Passover. At his last ritual meal with the Twelve he changed this Jewish feast into the sacrament or memorial of his death and resurrection (through which he makes a new covenant). From its institution the celebration of this memorial meal marks the dividing line between the new community and the old People of God. It forms the foundation of all the functions of the apostles and their successors: to teach, to govern, and to sanctify. The gathering of the disciples, especially the Twelve, had its celebration in view. It also forms the core of the eschatological existence of the Church. The memorial celebration will not only recall the memory of the resurrected Lord who has ascended into heaven but will also strengthen the hope and longing for his return in glory.[189] And finally, just like any other covenant, the new covenant has its terms or commandment. This is the commandment of love. Christ commands his followers to love God, to be united and love one another just as he himself has loved them (see Mt. 5-7). And this love is to be the hallmark of those who follow his ways (Jn. 13:34-35). The celebration of the Eucharist, then, without love is an abuse of the sacrament. Those who wish to celebrate it fruitfully must learn to love sincerely and in a sacrificial manner; they must be prepared to die for Christ or for the welfare of those he died to save.

(ii) Gathering the Disciples and the Twelve.

Another important act of Jesus in founding his Church is the gathering of the disciples. His gathering of his disciples calls to mind the men of the old covenant to whom were assigned special missions, especially the seventy elders who were given of the spirit of Moses (Num. 11:16-30). As we have shown before, Jesus himself freely and without pressure chose his disciples and he did not bind them to any particular school or tradition but to his person; they must be his disciples for ever.

The selection of the inner circle, the Twelve from the larger group of his disciples was one of the most important acts of Jesus' public ministry. Again, in the selection of the Twelve Jesus took the initiative and without any external human influence. He attached much importance to this selection. This inner circle which always remained with him was to be initiated into the mysteries of the kingdom of God. Jesus made time to teach them privately, even though they, like most other people, were also slow to understand Jesus and the mysteries he revealed (Mk. 4:40; 6:50-52 and par.). And, as was noted above, only they were allowed to take part in the Last Supper. The number, twelve was of special importance to the Israelites because of the twelve sons of Israel from which the twelve tribes sprang. The twelve apostles or simply the Twelve are a symbol of Israel and its fulfillment. (For it was Israel's expectation that at the messianic age the twelve tribes would be restored.) They are the patriarchs of the new Israel, the new People of God. By choosing twelve apostles Jesus implies that a new Israel, the new saving community is to arise. The apostles themselves understand the importance and implication of this number. That is why they have to replace Judas after he has committed suicide (Acts 1:15-26).

For these apostles Christ gives the mission of representing him, that is, taking his place in the world. The full power and authority which he received from the Father are transferred to them to continue his work on earth, although without their ceasing to be bound to him. He tells them. "As the Father has sent me, so I also send you" (Jn. 20:21). Whoever rejects his disciples rejects Christ, and whoever rejects him rejects God (Lk. 10:16). It is after his resurrection that Jesus commissions his apostles to be his witnesses, in Israel and the whole world. They all see the risen Lord after his resurrection. We have to note here that the title, *apostle,* is reserved for the Twelve and St. Paul, even though it may analogically be given to a pioneer missionary or evangelizer whose missionary activity played a great role in the conversion of some nation or territory.

The authority Jesus gives the apostles includes the power to bind and loose. Whatever they bind on earth will be considered bound in heaven: and whatever they consider loosed on earth will be considered loosed in heaven. This means that the apostles can declare something forbidden or permitted; they can impose an obligation or lift it, pronounce a decree (or ban) or remove it; exclude from the Church or readmit into it. This disciplinary authority gives the apostles in logical sequence teaching authority. The authority given them extends to the realm of conscience. Whatever they teach or maintain is accepted by God as his own teaching or decision. Obedience to them or the contrary is obedience or disobedience to God. And whatever sin they forgive, is forgiven by God and those they hold unforgiven are held by God as unforgiven (Jn. 20: 23). The confirmation by Jesus of his authority to his apostles after his resurrection is recorded in Matthew 28: 16-20. This statement has three parts. The first is the word of authorization which is the basis of other functions. Second, the command to teach and baptize. Finally, Christ promises to be with his apostles always till the end of time. This implies that this authority and promise was given not only to the apostles but also to their legitimate successors.

(iii) The Commission to Peter

The charge given the apostles receives its concentration and culmination in the authority given to Peter. In the Synoptic Gospels and Acts Peter is always listed first. In the gospels he is shown always as the spokesman for the rest, and is always the first to act. A few examples can illustrate this. Peter is the one who wants to bring back Jesus from solitude (Mk. 1:36). It is he who wants to preserve Jesus from death and has to be sternly rebuked for it (Mk. 8:32), who hastens on the waves to meet Jesus, walking on the waters (Mt.14: 28-32). He together with James and John form Jesus' intimate or innermost circle. The collectors of the temple tax turn to him and to no one else (Mt. 17:24f.). [190]

Three primary references in the Bible buttress Peter's special position or primacy among the apostles. These are Mt. 16:13-19; Lk. 22:31f; Jn. 21:15-19. According to Matthew's account, when Jesus inquires of the apostles as to their understanding of his identity, Simon Peter, as usual, is the first to answer. He confesses Jesus as the Messiah or the Christ ('Anointed One'), the son of the living God. Jesus observes that Peter's insight is not merely human knowledge but rather a revelation from God. He gives him the name *Peter* which means *rock,* and promises to build his saving community, the Church, on that rock. This is the leadership of or authority over the Church. No force opposed to God will be able to destroy this community. Jesus further promises to give to Peter the keys of the kingdom of heaven: whatever he binds/looses on earth will be considered bound/loosed in heaven. Here Jesus promises Peter to be the Prime Minister of the kingdom of God. For the keys are a symbol that Peter represents on earth the Master and owner of the house, namely Christ. And by the transfer of the keys, according to Hebrew and rabbinic language, he is installed as the deputy or Vicar of Christ. This can be understood better in the backdrop of its Old Testament antecedent. Isaiah (22:15-25) describes the establishment of Eliakim as the new Prime Minister of King Hezekiah of Judah. On his shoulder God places "the key of the House of David", and he has the authority to *shut* and to *open*. The words, *key,* to *shut* and to *open* are echoed in Christ's commissioning of Peter; as shown above, he has the power to bind and to loose. The authority given to Peter may include laying down rules or declaring them abrogated, imposing and lifting excommunications, forgiving or not forgiving sins, and the power to teach. In the passage of Matthew in which the commissioning of Peter is given, no distinction is made between *church* and *kingdom of heaven.* The power of the keys relates to the *kingdom of heaven.* And Jesus promises to build his *church* on Peter as rock. This does not mean that the Church and the kingdom of heaven or kingdom of God are identical. They, however, stand in very close connection, the Church being the beginning and instrument for bringing about the kingdom of God. Peter and other apostles open the door to the kingdom by proclamation, teaching, guidance and giving access to the Church. [191]

The commissioning of Peter recorded in Matthew 16:17-19, has been a subject of many debates from the time of Martin Luther, especially in the last decades of the nineteenth century. The reasons for objections to this passage containing the commissioning of Peter were that the account is not found in Mark and Luke and that the word *church* appearing there is unique in Jesus' tradition. Today, however, most Scripture scholars of both Catholic and Protestant denominations accept the genuineness of the passage, because they are convinced that Matthew preserved the older account of the Caesarea Philippi incident than Mark and Luke did, and they see that the text has thoroughly Aramaic tone, with such terms as *flesh and blood, Bar Jona,* and *bind/loose.* As to the word Jesus used in referring to his new community, scholars are of the view that even if Jesus did not use exactly the term *ecclesia or church* (supposing he used the term "my flock" or "my followers"), that does not take away from the text its genuineness or meaning. [192]

Another passage that refers to Peter's primacy is Lk.22:29-32. There is an argument among the apostles as to who is the greatest among them (Lk.22:24). After admonishing them on humility, Jesus promises to confer on them the kingdom which the Father

84

has conferred on him, and that they will sit on thrones judging the twelve tribes of Israel. Then he singles out Peter and warns him of Satan's plan to seriously shake the disciples. He informs Peter he has prayed for him so that he may retain his faith and strengthen his brethren. Jesus is aware that the devil will use the Passion to shake the faith of Peter and other disciples. His prayer is that Peter's faith may stand firm so that he may strengthen the Church (his brothers), for Peter's faith will be decisive for the growth and fall of all.[193]

According to John's Gospel, Jesus fulfills his promises to Peter after the resurrection. This testimony is the confirmation of Peter's position as head at this time when the Church is to continue Christ's work without him physically present. Christ prepared for the Church while historically or physically in the world. Now that he is about to leave, he gives over to that Church his work, with Peter as head. The passage in John (Jn. 21: 15-19) is the fulfillment of the promises recorded in Matthew and Luke. In John's record Jesus orders Peter to feed his lambs and his sheep.

Jesus' question to Peter put three times is not to be interpreted only as a reminder or repairing of Peter's denial. It is also a rite of installation or handing over of authority that was used there and then. In that rite the risen Jesus hands over to Peter the care of his new community or flock. We know the image of the sheep or flock and the shepherd appears many times in the Bible. The shepherd's function is to lead the flock, feed and protect it. Hence the psalmist claims the Lord as his shepherd (ps.23); and Jesus claims he is the good shepherd of his flock (Jn. 10). His role as shepherd he now transfers to Peter.[194]

Peter's unique or special position is confirmed by other passages in the New Testament, for instance in the Acts of the Apostles. Here Peter's first position is no longer a matter of promise; he is presented as having assumed his position as the spiritual leader of the nascent Church, as a courageous and successful proclaimer of the gospel, and as the guardian of the Church from dangers both within and without (cf. Acts 1:15-26; 2:14-40; 3:1-26; 4:8ff; 5:1-11; 5:29ff; 8:14-17; 8:18-25; 9:32-43). He was the first to break through the frontiers of Israel to reach the Gentiles. One of his most significant acts was the baptizing of the Gentile Cornelius and his entire house-hold, thereby crossing the boundary of Judaism and carrying the gospel to the Gentile world (Acts 10). Peter also played a decisive role in the first council of the Church, the Council of Jerusalem (Acts 15). By his speech there he brought about the decision not to impose on Gentile Christians the burden of circumcision which the Judaizers were insisting upon. From what we have seen so far in this chapter, it is clear that Jesus founded one Church which he intends to be the ordinary or usual way of salvation for all. The visible head of that Church was Peter, the first pope. The visible head of the Church today is the current pope who is the successor of Peter. And from Peter to the present pope there is an unbroken line of succession. Can any other religion or Christian denomination make that claim?

(iv) The Sending of the Spirit.

The process of the founding of the Church was completed with the coming of the Holy Spirit on the new community of Jesus. The view, or rather statement, that the Church was founded on Pentecost, must be understood in the backdrop of what has been stated above about the preparations Jesus made for establishing the Church and of his promise to send the Holy Spirit, that is, his Spirit on his followers, who were directed to remain in Jerusalem until they would receive this Spirit (ActsI:4-5). It may be clearer to state that Jesus made all the necessary preparations but the concrete realization of the arrangements or the official inauguration of the Church was on Pentecost Sunday. On that day, before a big assembly of the Jews, Peter, as the head of the apostles, bore witness to Christ as the Messiah long awaited by the Jews. And consequent upon the coming of the Spirit and Peter's preaching on that day, about three thousand people were added to the number of Christ's followers.

The Spirit's activity and Peter's preaching worked in cooperation on that day. Here is an example of the cooperation of divine activity and man's input in the life of the Church. And from that first Pentecost day on, the concrete shaping of the Church will be the work of the Spirit and human cooperation. Thus the Church in its concrete existence is the combination of the work of God and of man. It would be wrong to attribute it all to the Spirit or God alone. It would likewise be contradictory to the Scripture and to real life to exclude from the constitution of the Church the historical character of human activity. The Spirit on his coming gives the apostles a right understanding of Jesus and his work, which until now they do not properly understand. It is the Spirit who reveals to them the mystery of Christ and the meaning of the kingdom of God which he proclaimed. After his coming they are able to recognize Jesus Christ in the light of the Scripture as the Messiah sent by God (cf. Acts 2:25-35; 3:13-25; 4:11-12, 24-28; 10:36-43). Peter's preaching on Pentecost is an illustration of this. The Spirit also gives to the apostles extraordinary courage to bear witness for Christ even in the face of threats and torture. He also reveals to the hearers the meaning of the witness of the apostles, helps them to be converted and baptized. The result of the presence of the Spirit is the flourishing of the fledgling church described in the Acts of the Apostles. The power of the Spirit in the life of the early members of the Church, especially in their love for one another, is so much that they are described as having one heart and one soul. This helped in deepening the foundation of the Church at the early stage of its history. [195]

Before we continue, it will be helpful to sum up some of the ground we have covered in our discussion of the creation or foundation of the new People of God or rather the Church. Owing to his covenant with Abraham, God chose the people of Israel and saved them from Egypt and the Red Sea. He entered a covenant with them at Sinai. By this covenant they belonged to God in a special way; they became the People of God. Through them God intended to save the human race. They on their part were expected to remain faithful to the terms of the covenant, which essentially consisted in serving God alone and depending on him. The Israelites, however, despite repeated warnings of the prophets, consistently broke their covenant with God. As a result of this, God promised to make a new covenant. This new covenant was at last ratified or sealed with the blood of Jesus Christ the Son of God. Through it a new People of God, or rather a new family of God which inherits the promises made to the patriarch Abraham, was created. For this new community, at his last Passover meal, Christ instituted a new paschal meal, the memorial or re-enactment of his death and resurrection, which for them now supplants the Jewish Passover meal. This new paschal meal is the Eucharist.

To ensure the continuity of this new people, Jesus chose his disciples or followers. From this larger group he chose an inner circle, the twelve apostles who represented the restored twelve tribes of Israel. He commissioned them to continue his work on earth. Yet from the Twelve he chose one man to be the head of his new community and his vicar on earth. This head and Vicar of Christ was Peter. To him and the Church of which he is the visible head are given the keys of the kingdom of heaven, the complete means of salvation. After the resurrection of Jesus and after his Spirit had descended on his followers, the apostles took over the work of Jesus of proclaiming the good news of the kingdom of God as he commanded. As is evident in the Acts of the Apostles and some other New Testament writings, Peter at this time immediately assumed his function as leader of the young Church.

The apostles in their turn, to ensure the same continuity of the new community of Christ, toward the end of their lives, appointed their successors to whom they handed over the authority and mission which Jesus had given them. As was laid down by these apostles, the successors in turn were to appoint and hand over to their own successors and so on until the end of time. Thus the apostolic tradition has been preserved and handed on by those who were made bishops by the apostles and their successors. And just as the office or function which Jesus entrusted to Peter alone as head of the apostles, destined to be handed on without interruption to his successors, is to last until the end of time, so also the office the apostles received as shepherds of the flock of Christ is permanent and has been taken over by the bishops of the Church who are their legitimate successors. [196]

The Catholic Church has all the features we have discussed, namely, the Eucharist, the successor of Peter or the pope, and the sacred order of bishops in full communion with him. Hence it claims that the church founded by Jesus Christ "continues fully only in the Catholic Church," and that other churches and ecclesial communities "derive their efficacy from the very fullness of grace and truth entrusted to the Catholic Church."[197] This is to say that while the Catholic Church admits that other churches and ecclesial communities, especially those that have valid Eucharist and episcopate, may have some means of salvation, these means are found fully only in the Catholic Church.[198] This is the meaning of the statement that the Catholic Church is the religion founded by God himself through Christ as the ordinary way of salvation for the human race. It is no wonder then it is called "a sign and instrument . . . of communion with God."[199]

"Outside the Church there is no Salvation"

Owing to this unique role given to the Catholic Church, there arose during the time of the Fathers of the Church, specifically in the time of Saint Cyprian, the maxim, "Outside the Church there is no salvation."[200] This saying was often used by Catholics before the Council of Trent. Today conservative Evangelicals, found mainly in mainline Protestant churches and sometimes in the Catholic Church, still hold that view. In this view salvation is not possible in non-Christian religions. It maintains that for anyone to be saved he must have a personal faith experience of Jesus as Lord and only savior.[201]

Karl Barth's teaching on salvation in non-Christian religions is a good representation of the position of most conservative Evangelicals on this issue.[202] Karl Barth clearly rejects the possibility of salvation in non-Christian religions.[203] He sees religion in general as man's futile attempt to sanctify and save himself. Only the Christian religion, according to him, is the locus of true and salvific religion.[204] All other religions are unbelief. Barth proceeds to explain his stand.

His starting point is God's revelation made in Jesus Christ as contained in the Bible. He sees this as not only the only starting point but also the end point of his approach and of those who are serious about attaining the salvation God intends for them. He points out that there are two elements in revelation, which make it quite clear that "religion" is unbelief. The first is that only God can reveal God. For revelation is God's "self-manifestation" which confronts man "on the presupposition and confirmation of the fact that man's attempts to know God from his own standpoint are but wholly and entirely futile."[205] Barth thus rejects all human attempts to know God. He emphatically states that with regard to knowing God, all human activity is in vain even in the best life.[206] Citing several passages from the New Testament, he tries to explain that there is a God-given potential in every human person, but that this potential, the potential to know God, is never actualized except through revelation in Christ. [207]

From the foregoing Barth states a corollary; that is, only God can save man, just as only God can reveal God. We are saved by grace alone. In Barth's view each time people attempt by themselves to know God or find salvation they fall into the sin of rebellion against God; only God can save man and he has done so only in Jesus Christ.[208] Man's effort to save himself is what Barth regards as "religion" and he sees it as unbelief: "Religion is unbelief. It is a concern; indeed, we must say that it is the one great concern, of godless man."[209]

The Christian religion is not free from Barth's judgment of religions. This religion, according to him, empirically, in itself, its human origin and practice, has nothing which shows it is different from or better than other religions. For, as a religion it shares in the same sin of idolatry, of self-righteousness, unbelief. Having made this judgment Barth employs the Reformation theology for the forgiveness of sin (which demands only "faith alone" in order to be justified) to justify the Christian religion. It does not deserve in itself to be the true religion. It is the true religion only by divine election, and because its sins have been freely forgiven by God, "in virtue of the divine justification of sinners, of the divine forgiveness of sins." It is justified by God by imputation through the righteousness of Christ.[210]

Barth speaks of Christianity as the true religion in the way the Reformers speak of a justified sinner. His argument here is that, just as a human being who is a sinner, despite his natural sinfulness, and owing to his faith in Jesus Christ, can be accepted and saved by God, so also Christianity, despite its unworthiness and owing to its belief in Christ, has been justified or accepted as the true religion by God. It is, therefore, justified not of its own being or nature;[211] it is justified *sola gratia*, by grace alone, only by God's gratuitous offer of justification. This means God accepts this religion by imputing to it the righteousness of Christ.[212]

This argument if stated simply is this: there can be only one true religion, that is, the Christian religion because revelation and salvation are offered only in Jesus Christ. And hence Christianity is justified in such a way that Barth affirms nothing of other religions. It is only in its close connection with the human nature of Christ that the Christian religion is called the true religion. Barth stresses this point. "The divine fact of the name of Jesus Christ confirms what no other fact does or can confirm: the creation and election of this religion to be the one and only true religion."[213] The Christian religion, then, does not have any value apart from its connection with Jesus Christ. This connection and only it gives this religion advantage over other religions: its meaning and value flowing there from.[214]

It is clear by now that the one point Barth (with other conservative Evangelicals) insists upon is that thanks to its close connection with the person or name of Jesus Christ Christianity is the only true and justified religion, that is, the only religion which is a means of salvation. Other religions no matter how good or true they might appear, are false and useless: there can be no salvation in them because they cannot bear the name of Jesus Christ.[215]

On other extreme is the position of contemporary liberal theologians from the Catholic and Protestant churches. These theologians endorse the current positive attitude of the Catholic Church toward non-Christian religions as a good gesture, though they see it as not going far enough, as inadequate. In their desire to foster a greater spirit of dialogue with non-Christian religions they tend to make all religions, Christianity included, relative; for them there is no difference between non-Christian religions and the Christian religion as a way of salvation. We shall understand better the position of this group by considering briefly its most vocal representative, John Hick.[216]

John Hick was formerly an Evangelical. In his book, *God Has Many Names,* he narrates how his experiences in various non-Christian communities in England completely changed his former attitude or rather made him undergo another conversion to liberalism. He advocates a similar change in other Evangelicals.[217]

Hick sees no difference between Christianity and non—Christian religions. For him different religions are various human responses to the one divine reality. Hence he considers it inappropriate to ask which is the true religion. "For a true relation-ship to God may occur in the lives of people in each of the great religious traditions."[218] He locates the birth of these great religions in the period between roughly 900 and 200 B. C., when in different parts of the world appeared charismatic individuals who became the founders of these great religions. The fact that these religions had developed in isolation from each other made each of them think it was the only one hence to claim to he the only true religion. Yet the religion that lays the greatest claim to absoluteness is Christianity, one of the "major new developments within the stream of Semitic monotheism that was formed by the Hebrew prophets."[219] Traditional Christianity, in Hick's view, like the sun, places itself in the center of the universe of religions around which all the religions of the world must rotate and must be evaluated. He, therefore, proposes what he calls a "Copernican revolution" in the Christian theology of religions. This revolution has to bring about the shift from the conviction that the Christian religion is at the center to "the thought that it is God who is at the center and all the religions of mankind, including our own, serve and revolve around him."[220] For Hick this means placing Christian on equal par with other religions without any distinction whatever.

In his attempt to reduce the Christian religion to the same level as other religions, Hick realizes that he faces a very strong obstacle, namely, the fact that Christians believe that Jesus is God. This belief, in Hick's view, leads Christians to make a number of conclusions: first from the conclusion that only their religion is founded by God in person to "the further conclusion that he must want all his human children to be related to him through this religion which he has himself founded for us."[221] To overcome this great obstacle Hick resorts to the rhetoric of Arius, denying that Jesus is metaphysically divine. He assigns Christ only a mythological or poetic epithet of divinity.[222] Jesus, says Hick, did not consider himself God or God incarnate. The "New Testament scholarship", he says, "has shown how fragmentary and ambiguous are the data available" about Jesus, a "historical individual who lived in Galilee in the first third of the first century of the Christian era."[223] He is of the view that the idea of the divinity of Jesus Christ was projected on Jesus by Christians in the early history of Christianity and that "in the new age of world ecumenism" it is important for Christians to be aware of "the mythological character of this traditional language."[224] Further, he compares the attribution of divinity to Jesus to the exaltation to a divine figure of Gautama by Mahayana Buddhists, members of the religious tradition founded by Gautama.[225]

Hick, however, concedes that the resurrection of Jesus makes the difference between the ascription of divinity to him and the exaltation of Gautama. Yet, he is of the opinion that Jesus is not the only person who has risen from the dead, and that the resurrection therefore is not a guarantee or very firm basis for attributing divinity to him. Here Hick reveals one of the main sources of his error and of other liberal theologians about the divinity of Christ. They confuse resurrection with raising back to mortal life of a dead body or re-animation of a corpse. Hick, for instance, mentions instances which he considers to be resurrections similar to that of Jesus; some of these are the cases of raising to life of Lazarus (Jn. 11: 1-44), the widow's son (Lk. 7: 11-17), Jairus's daughter (Mk. 5:35-43 and par.). He therefore asserts that the resurrection of Jesus "did not automatically put him in quite a unique category": that is, that the resurrection of Jesus does not necessarily show him to be unique or divine.[226] But in the last chapter we learned that resurrection is not the same thing as waking up back to our mortal life after dying.

It is important here to point out that John Hick and the liberal theologians he represents are right in holding that different religions are different human responses to the same divine reality. But they err by not seeing any real difference between the Christian religion and other religions. For them all these other religions are as good as Christianity as a way of salvation and salvation can be found apart from Christ. Hick puts it succinctly: "We can say that there is salvation in Christ without having to say that there is no salvation other than in Christ."[227] This position is too liberal and unacceptable to the Catholic Church. Nor does the Church espouse the view of conservative Evangelicals represented by Karl Barth. This group rightly holds that the close connection between the Christian religion and the person of Jesus Christ sets this religion off from other religions. But it too errs by going too far the opposite direction in ruling out completely the possibility of salvation in non-Christian religions. This position also is unacceptable to the Catholic Church because it is too extreme.

The Catholic Church today explains the implications of the statement "outside the Church there is no salvation." The statement must first all be understood as applying to Christ; for there is no salvation except through Christ as has been explained before. It applies also to the Church, the historical continuation of Christ or his sacrament, which Christ himself has instituted as the ordinary means of salvation as we have shown above. Therefore basing its teaching on the Holy Scripture and tradition, the Church today insists on its necessity; that it is necessary for salvation. To be saved one has to be, at least some how, associated or related with the Church of Christ which "subsists in the Catholic Church", governed by the pope and the bishops in communion with him.[228] For Christ, the one mediator of salvation, who is present in the Church, his mystical body, taught that the Church is necessary for salvation. This the Second Vatican Council states thus: "Hence they could not be saved who, knowing the Catholic Church was founded as necessary by God through Christ, would refuse either to enter it, or to remain in it."[229] Having said this, the council goes further to point out those who belong to the Church and those related to it.

Those who fully belong to the Church are sincere Catholics who accept all the means of salvation offered by the Catholic Church (which alone has the complete means of salvation) and "are joined in the visible structure of the Church of Christ who rules through the Supreme Pontiff and the bishops." But being baptized Catholic is not enough. To qualify for true membership in the Church and for salvation one must remain a good Catholic, practicing his faith which is illustrated by his practice of Christian charity. Catechumens who desire to be full members of the Church also belong to the Church.[230] Other Christians who are properly baptized and belong to the churches or ecclesial bodies not in full communion with the Catholic Church have the respect of the Church. They are "put in some, though imperfect, communion with the Catholic Church."[231] The closest to the Catholic Church among these churches are the Eastern churches or rather the Eastern Orthodox Churches.[232] And finally are those who are related to the church in various ways. These are non-Christians of good will whom we shall describe below. Thus those who are non-Catholics in good faith and non-Christians, who through no fault of their own have not received the message of Christ in a convincing way, are not included among those who cannot gain salvation outside the Church.

Salvation in Non-Christian Religions

As we have just hinted above, the Church today sees all non-Christians of good will to be related to the Christian economy or the salvation won by Christ. These non-Christians are enumerated in a descending order, in the order of their closeness to the Church. Those who do not acknowledge Jesus Christ as God but are of good will are seen as ordained or related to the Church in various ways. The first are the Jews who are the people "to which the covenants and promises were made, and from which Christ was born according to the flesh". Following immediately are Moslems "who profess to hold the faith of Abraham, and together with us they adore the one, merciful God, mankind's judge on the last day". All other non-Christians who through no fault of their own have not become Christians, but who "seek God with a sincere heart, and, moved by grace, try in their actions to do his will as they know it through the dictates of their conscience" may also gain eternal salvation.[233]

The Church thus sees all non-Christians of good will related in various ways to God's plan of salvation in Christ. As can be seen in the preceding paragraph there is a gradation in this relationship or rather the relations exist at different levels. First, there is the relation with the Jews, then with Moslems. After these two groups, which with the Christian religion maintain absolute monotheism and claim the patriarch Abraham as their father, come other non-Christian religions.

But to understand better what the Church means by these favorable statements about the various non-Christians it may be helpful to understand the meaning of the expression "non-Christians of good will" which the Church uses often in its statements. And we often also hear the expression "men of good will". What do these expressions mean? For the understanding of the meaning of *men of good will or people of good will* we have to understand first what the human person is. What is man?

Meaning of Man

Philosophers define man or the human person as *a rational animal.* This is a very derogatory definition of the human person. Man or the human person is far more than that. Those who use only human reason in considering or defining the human person fall short of the true understanding of what man really is. The revelation that comes through Jesus Christ is very crucial for a true and adequate understanding of the meaning of man.

It is the teaching of Scripture that God loves all human beings and wishes everyone to be saved (Acts 10: 35; 1 Tim. 2:4). But God did not stop at wishing it; he formed every human being in such a way that he can tend to salvation, tend to reaching the beatific vision by accepting God's self-communication or God's offer of himself to man in grace. For in planning to pour forth the love which is himself, in planning to communicate himself, God creates man, making him in such a way that he can receive this love, God himself, as a gratuitous gift. Man should always have the potency or capacity for this love, the capacity for God.[234] In real concrete human existence, thanks to the universal salvific plan of God, there is no 'pure nature' in any human being; that is to say, there is no human person who does not have in his nature this capacity for God in grace.[235]

As was stated in the last chapter, the Incarnation or God's becoming of man in Jesus can tell us much about human nature, about what man is. Jesus as man is the self-utterance or self-expression of God. Now, if God has become man in the person of Jesus, then man or the human person is that which takes place when God expresses himself. The human person can be defined as that which happens when God expresses himself *ad extra,* in the region outside the divine. This is to say that since man's nature is equal to Jesus' human nature in its *quiddity* or essence, it follows that man's nature is a possible self-expression of God—if God wishes to communicate himself *ad extra* or in the region outside the divine. The very fact that God has assumed human nature in the man Jesus explains what man is: the emptiness into which God could empty himself. Jesus the God-man is God's explanation of what man is. In a word, only through the incarnation of God in Jesus, who shares the same human nature as every other human being, can we understand what human nature really is.[236] Hence the Church says, "In reality it is only in the mystery of the Word made flesh that the mystery of man truly becomes clear." The Church goes on to explain: "Human nature, by the very fact that it was assumed, not absorbed, in him, has been raised in us also to a dignity beyond compare." This implies that by his assuming of our nature, human nature, Christ has revealed to us the unbelievably great height to which God has raised man, every human being. But that is not all: by his incarnation too. Jesus, "the son of God, has in a certain way, united himself to every human person."[237]

Human nature then *is* made by God in such a way that it can receive God's self-expression or self-communication. It has a capacity or potency for God. This potency has the characteristic of a spiritual dynamism to seek God or rather tend toward God. (That is why every human person is somehow spiritual.) This spiritual elevation of the human person enabling him to move or tend by his spiritual dynamism toward God, a dynamism which has God also as its efficient cause, has the nature of a revelation, though not in the sense of a verbal revelation or in the form of verbal proposition. It is rather a revelation in the sense of change of awareness or consciousness originating from God's antecedent self-communication or self-donation in grace. Man cannot refuse this revelation or rather the antecedent self-communication of God without contradicting himself, his very being, since this gift is already a constituent of his very essence. If man accepts that revelation which is the same as accepting himself, he accepts God and hence can be saved.[238] A man who thus accepts God by accepting this interior and antecedent revelation is a man usually guided by his conscience. Until the gospel message has been convincingly presented to him he can gain Christian salvation, the salvation won by Christ, even before he officially or explicitly joins the Church. He is a man of good will included by the Church among those who "seek God with a sincere heart" and who "try in their actions to do his will as they know it through the dictates of their conscience."[239]

We must remember here, however, that a person properly guided by his conscience is one who has a good conscience, which is a conscience proximately guided by right reason and ultimately by the will of God. But experience has shown that owing to various circumstances, not all human beings have this type of conscience. There are different kinds of conscience that are misleading and people who have them are many among both Christians and non-Christians. Even people who have the right conscience, often in their lives, need positive instructions or directives as to the best thing to do to please God or attain ultimate peace or salvation. The uniqueness of the Christian religion is that God himself, seeing the human predicament, has, in Jesus Christ, come in person to show everybody the right way, or rather, to be the guide or the way to salvation.[240]

The Church today admits that men of good will, who have not come into convincing contact with the gospel, can get help for their salvation through observing what is good or authentic in their religions. According to the Church God, in his own good pleasure, can bring about the salvation of non-Christians of good will (those who through no fault of their own have not become Christians) by their "sincere practice of what is good in their own religious traditions."[241] Some people who do not follow the teaching of the Catholic Church may object to this. Such people should pause and think. What about people who live naturally good lives (in pre-Christian cultures or epochs), following their conscience, but who have never come in convincing contact with the Church or the gospel? Surely God will not deprive such people of salvation.[242] The argument may be that baptism is not administered to such people, which is necessary for salvation. Again, it has been the teaching of the Church for many years that people who sincerely desire baptism and fail to receive it before they die can receive the baptism of desire which for them is sufficient. People who follow their conscience but have not had convincing contact with the gospel are presumed to have that implicit desire for baptism; they can attain salvation.[243] The salvation thus given to such non-Christians is the salvation won by Christ, for there is no other salvation. All those who are saved share in the one mystery of Christ through the Holy Spirit. For Christ died and rose for the salvation of all. And that is why the Church further says, "since all men are in fact called to one and the same destiny, which is divine, we must hold that the Holy Spirit offers to all the possibility of being made partners, in the way known to God, in the paschal mystery."[244] Because of the possibility of the activities of the Holy Spirit in non-Christian religions, the Church reminds its missionaries to always bear in mind that they are not operating in a complete void. The non-Christians to whom the message of salvation is being preached "may in many cases have already responded implicitly to God's offer of salvation in Jesus Christ."[245] This response could be done in the way pointed out above.

But as indicated before, we must also always bear in mind that the non-Christians who can be saved by the means mentioned in this part of the chapter are those who through no fault of their own have not come into convincing contact with the message of Christ or his Church. While the Church admits the possibility of salvation in non-Christian religions, this possibility is regarded as the extra-ordinary way which God in his omnipotence can use whenever he wills. The ordinary or usual way of salvation which he has given to the human race, as we have shown above, is the Catholic Church. If some means of salvation are found in their minute beginnings in non-Christian religions, they are found in complete form in the Catholic Church. What is found in its first beginnings in the one is found in complete form in the other. All things being equal, a Christian has a far better chance to be saved than a non-Christian because of the reasons that have been given. This understanding puts the responsibility or burden on Christians to proclaim the message to the Whole world with all the means available; to present the message of Christ to all in a convincing way, so that they may explicitly accept the faith and have a better chance of being saved.

CHAPTER SEVEN

THE URGENCY OF PROCLAMATION

Jesus is the only savior of the whole human race, as has already been made clear. We have noted also that the Church is the ordinary way of salvation given by God to the human race and the sacrament or continued presence of Christ in the world. As such a sacrament, it must appear in every part of the world at all times as the historical tangibility of God's saving love. It must therefore proclaim the gospel; it must evangelize everywhere and at all times, in order to appear thus. This is the first Christological foundation of evangelization or rather proclamation. The second is rooted in Christ's command. Jesus Christ, who said the purpose of his coming to this world was to proclaim the good news of the kingdom of God (Lk. 4:43) and who did in fact make that his main earthly ministry, mandated his Church to spread the same good news of the kingdom or salvation to every part of the world and to seek the conversion of all to Christianity, which he himself has founded as the way of salvation for all (cf. Mt. 28:16-20; Mk.16:15-16; Acts. 1:8).[246] The Church is therefore by nature missionary: it was founded to make disciples of all nations and will cease to be church if it stops proclaiming the message of salvation.

Aware of this truth and obligation, the Catholic Church from the Second Vatican Council to the present, while admitting that God in ways known to himself can lead to salvation those who through no fault of their own have not been converted to Christ, has consistently maintained the necessity of proclamation. It rightly holds that it "has the obligation and also the sacred right" to proclaim the gospel, to carry on missionary activity. For "by this missionary activity God is fully glorified, when men fully and consciously accept the work of salvation which he accomplished in Christ."[247] Many statements similar to this have appeared in several Church documents since the end of the Second Vatican Council. For instance the working paper of the 1974 Synod of Bishops states that "evangelization for which the Church is sent by the will of Christ, constitutes the essential task of the Church and its raison d'être.[248] But the most important documents about proclamation issued since the council are Pope Paul VI's *Evangelii Nuntiandi* and Pope John Paul II's *Redemptoris Missio*. *Evangelii Nuntiandi* published on December 8, 1975, the tenth anniversary of the end of the Second Vatican Council, makes it clear that proclamation is not something the Church can undertake or overlook at its own discretion but rather a duty imposed on it by its Lord and founder Jesus Christ for the salvation of the world. The document insists that the Christian message of salvation which is necessary and irreplaceable does not admit "of any indifference, of any accommodation to the principles of other religious beliefs, for on it depends the whole issue of man's salvation and in it are contained all the splendors of divine revelation."[249]

Anticipating such objections as to whether proclamation would not endanger the Church's dialogue with non-Christian religions, the document replies that "neither our respect for these religions nor the high esteem in which we hold them should deter the church from proclaiming" the gospel message to them. It maintains that non-Christians have the right to hear of the riches of the Christ-event through which alone salvation was given to the world; and that in these riches the whole human race can find in complete form and beyond all expectations everything for which adherents of other religions "have been groping, as it were, about man and his ultimate destiny, about life and death and about truth itself." With this statement the document thus stresses the uniqueness and necessity of the Christian message. While followers of other religions are groping about in search of salvation, the Christian religion offers this salvation freely in its full form in Jesus Christ. Then *Evangelii Nuntiandi* makes this even clearer and indicates too the uniqueness of the Church with the following statement, "By virtue of our religion a true and living relationship with God is established which other religions cannot achieve."[250] Here lies the great difference between the Christian religion and other religions. While it is possible to attain salvation in non-Christian religions, the possibility is even greater, all things being equal, in the Church, which has the full means of salvation and through it can be established "a true and living relationship with God" which is not possible in other religions. Why is this possible only in the Church? Because, as has been said several times before, the Church is the continued presence of Jesus Christ, the God-man, in the world; it is the religion founded by God himself through Jesus Christ, the God-man. Here man is no longer groping or searching for God. On the contrary, God himself has come down in search of man and leads him on the way of salvation.

A similar position is taken by Pope John Paul II's *Redemptoris Missio* which says that the "urgency of missionary activity derives from the radical newness of life brought by Christ", the only savior of the whole human race,[251] and in whom God has inaugurated on earth his kingdom which Jesus proclaimed during his earthly ministry. It is his resurrection through which Jesus now "shares in God's power and in his dominion over the world", maintains this document, that gives urgency and "a universal scope to Christ's message."[252]

It should be clear then that the Catholic Church still rightly maintains that proclamation of the gospel message is necessary today. It sees the latter as its raison d'être or mainstay, so that it will cease to exist as church if it stops proclaiming the message. It would be failing in its duty if it were to belittle the proclamation of the gospel to the whole world. Its dialogue with non-Christian religions, therefore, is not a substitute for proclamation. Next we shall consider the meaning of proclamation within the wider context of evangelization.

Proclamation within the Context of Evangelization

To understand or appreciate the importance of proclamation, we must consider it within the wider context of evangelization: we should first describe very briefly the meaning of evangelization. Evangelization itself is Christ's earthly ministry or mission, which is now taken over by the Church, the historical continuation of his presence or sacrament in the world. But can it be synonymous with any of the following: proclamation of Christ to those who do not know him, catechetics, baptism, or administration of other sacraments? True, all these are aspects of evangelization but they do not individually or collectively exhaust the meaning of the term.[253] Evangelization is a very broad term and embraces a lot of the activities of the Church. How then can we describe it here, at least in some limited way? It has to be understood as "the carrying forth of the *good* news to every sector of the human race so that by its strength it may enter into the hearts of men and renew the human race." Its aim is to bring about interior transformation both in individuals and the communities in which they live. The Church evangelizes, then, when by means of the gospel message it proclaims, it "seeks to convert both the individual consciences of men and their collective conscience, all the activities in which they are engaged and, finally, their lives and the whole environment which surrounds them."[254] The aim of evangelization then is not to destroy the culture or what the people hold dear but to transform and convert individuals, their environment and their society; "to effect and, as it were, recast the criteria of judgment, the standard of values, and life standards of the human race which are inconsistent with the word of God and the plan of salvation."[255] Thus evangelization must have as its ultimate goal conversion or transformation along the lines of the gospel message.

Proclamation and Other Relevant Dimensions of Evangelization

Effective proclamation of the gospel message involves several dimensions of evangelization. Initial conversion and subsequent growth of the faith is often brought about or aided by some of these dimensions of evangelization working together. The first of these is *witness:* bringing the message of Christ is first of all bearing witness to the good news revealed by him. This witness may be the first clear revelation of God to some or rather an aid for them to explicitate their implicit belief: it may be making clear to them the knowledge of the God they adore without knowing him. Evangelization must also include *proclamation* which is always its heart and without which the message that witness endeavors to give may not be quite clear. This means that evangelization must include the declaration that in Jesus Christ salvation is offered to everyone. Thirdly it must take into consideration the cultural values of the people to whom the good news is proclaimed; that is to say, the incarnation of the Church or *inculturation* is a very important part of evangelization.[256] Though there are several other dimensions of evangelization, these three form the central or essential dimensions. We shall now consider each of these in a little more detail in order to make clear what is required for effective proclamation of the good news.

(i) Witness

The Church always stresses the importance of witness in spreading the good news. This is especially true since the Second Vatican Council. A number of documents have been issued in this regard. A few examples will make this clear. In *Ad Gentes* the council directs Christians to show, wherever they are, by the example of their lives and the testimony of the word, that life of grace and the power of the Holy Spirit which they received when they became the people of God through the sacraments of initiation. Their actions are to speak louder than their words to non-Christians. To bear witness they must "establish the relationship of respect and love" with the people among whom they live and work, identify themselves as part and parcel of the group they live in, and as much as possible share in their cultural and social life.[257] Christian witness should always be animated by disinterested Christian charity, which knows no distinction of race, social standing or religion. Thus through its members, the Church like Christ himself, associates itself with human beings in every condition, though it gives special preference to the poor and those in need, sharing their joys and sorrows.[258]

However, many Christians have failed in this and other ways and consequently have failed to present the Church and the gospel in good light among non-Christians. This, *Gaudium et Spes* of the Second Vatican laments. It sees as a weakening factor in the spreading of the gospel the discrepancy between the message the Church proclaims and the human weakness of Christians, especially many of those who commit themselves to preaching the gospel. The document therefore admonishes Christians to renew and purify themselves, so that "the sign of Christ may shine more brightly over the face of the Church". Bishops and priests are "to build up by their daily behavior and concern an image of the Church capable of impressing men with the power and truth of the Christian message". Not only by their preaching the gospel message but even more by the witness of their lives they have to help the faithful to see the light of the gospel shine in their own daily activities. In other words, by what they say and what they do, the clergy have to prepare the laity for spreading the good news. The laity on their part must take seriously their temporal responsibilities integrating into them their religious conviction in such a way that their faith can easily be seen in their work. With their conscience properly formed, they are "to impress the divine law on the affairs of the earthly city". Thus through the witness of the life of Christians, the clergy and the laity alike, as well as the guidance of the Holy Spirit, the Church will be seen for what it really is: an unfailing "sign of salvation in the world."[259] This will help proclamation to be more fruitful.

Pope Paul VI's *Evangelii Nuntiandi* and Pope John Paul II's *Redemptoris Missio* also stress the necessity of witness in evangelization. The former envisages Christians as people who in the places they live and work will radiate "simply and spontaneously their faith in values which transcend common values and their hopes in things which are not seen". Such silent witness which will arouse among non-Christians curiosity or inquiry about the Church is seen as constituting a very effective form of evangelization. Since it arouses interest or curiosity among non-Christians, it is seen as the first step in evangelization.[260] This importance of witness in evangelization makes it necessary for the Church and Christians to be more and more like Christ in their life; to be close to the author of life and of evangelization. This is one of the reasons the document stresses the Christological foundation of evangelization: evangelization is Christ's work done on his behalf by the Church, and to be effective the Church must be close to Christ; it must constantly be evangelized itself, must be continually converted or renewed.[261] The document takes seriously Christ's warning, "apart from me you can do nothing" (Jn. 15:5); evangelization cannot really exist without union with Christ.

Redemptoris Missio stresses the same point. It puts it succinctly: "people today put more trust in witnesses than in teachers, in experience than in teaching, and in life and action than in theories. The witness of a Christian life is the first and irreplaceable form of mission." One of the most convincing forms of witness is disinterested concern for people, especially the poor. Why is it convincing? Because it "stands in marked contrast to human selfishness", to the greed and egocentricism of the spirit of this world.[262] Selfless service given to those in need can enable the Church to bear witness in other ways such as challenging corruption and oppressive political and economic systems. Pope John Paul II enumerates the ways in which the Church and its missionaries can bear witness. It is the duty of the Church to bear selfless witness to Christ "by taking courageous and prophetic stands in the face of the corruption of political and economic power". It must not seek its own glory or material gain but rather has to use its own resources to "serve the poorest of the poor" and thus imitate Christ's simplicity of life. The pontiff makes it clear that it is necessary for both the Church and its missionaries to subject themselves to personal and collective "examination of conscience in order to correct in their behavior whatever is contrary to the gospel and disfigures the face of Christ".[263]

(ii) Proclamation

But witness alone, says the Church, is not enough; for no matter how good it is, witness may be vague in the message it gives unless it is clarified by proclamation. The pride of place of the latter in evangelization is evidenced by the fact that sometimes evangelization is identified with proclamation, even though it is only one part of it. "Just as the whole economy of salvation has its center in Christ, so too all missionary activity is directed to the proclamation of his mystery."[264] In this chapter we shall sometimes use proclamation and evangelization interchangeably. For any effort worth the name of evangelization must proclaim the message of Jesus Christ. And in the mind of the Church evangelization or rather proclamation must have conversion culminating in entry into the Church and active participation in the Church's life as its ultimate aim. This aim sets it off from other activities such as inter-religious dialogue strictly speaking and mere philanthropic engagements. That goal or aim too can help many missionaries solve some of the problems or questions that they often meet. For instance, is a Christian teaching biology in a high school in Saudi Arabia or Iran an evangelizer or rather missionary? Or can a Christian nurse working in a general hospital in Kuwait or Pakistan be regarded as a missionary? The determining factor, according to the Church, is always the ultimate aim. Are these Christians working to earn their living and at the same time providing a silent Christian presence without the least desire to convert anyone? Or are they working as philanthropists? Both these motives are good and praiseworthy, but in the mind of the Church these Christians are not evangelizers, if they do not at least have the desire to bring those among whom they are working nearer to Christ, that is to say, if they do not have the intention to convert anyone. For anyone therefore to qualify as an evangelizer or missionary, he must help in some way in the Church's missionary effort, or at least have the desire to do so. If his work is his Christian witness it needs to be clarified by proclamation. For, says the Church, "the meaning of a person's witness will be clarified by preaching, clearly and unambiguously, the Lord Jesus."[265]

Though a part of proclamation, namely catechetics, often uses instruction, proclamation should not be reduced to mere teaching or rather simply intellectual information. This in itself usually does not convert people. It must follow Jesus' pattern of proclamation: it must be presented as the nearness of God, the nearness of salvation. What authentic proclamation says is: God's power and salvation are now available for you to draw upon; make use of the opportunity: reach out and take hold of the salvation offered to you now. It is not always easy for the missionary to make this proclamation. Often his own faith is challenged in hostile or difficult situations. He must, however, remember always that as a representative of the Church, he is working with the mandate of and in union with the Church and also with the Holy Spirit, the guide of missionaries. [266]

The Message to Be Proclaimed

While other elements of the gospel message may be left out, change or be modified according to the changing circumstances the central or core elements must always be present in every genuine proclamation. What are these indispensable core elements?

First, the message to be proclaimed is about the God revealed by Jesus Christ. In other words, it must be about God the almighty creator of heaven and earth. But it must emphasize that God is not an anonymous force or power; that he is our father, the true father of the whole human race who loves the world in Jesus Christ his Son through whom he created all things and calls all human beings to eternal life.[267]

Secondly the message of salvation must have as its "foundation, the center and the apex of its whole dynamic power, this explicit declaration: in Jesus Christ who became man, died and rose again from the dead salvation is offered" to every human being as a gratuitous gift from God. This salvation is not simply earthly or material salvation but essentially the self-donation of God to man or rather the union of man with God which begins in this life as the life of grace and continues in the hereafter as the beatific vision.[268]

Since the salvation offered to man in Christ is essentially transcendent and otherworldly, the message has to include a prophetic proclamation of the life to come, man's eternal vocation which is connected with, though distinct from, his present state. This vocation transcends earthly life and history and goes to the true destiny of man which will be revealed in the hereafter. Proclamation must, therefore, be good news, a gospel of hope founded on the promises made by God in the new covenant through the one mediator between God and mankind, Jesus Christ. It has to include love; first of all God's love for us and also our love for God, which love is our motivating force in having sincere love for other people, since we are all sons and daughters of the one God in whose image and likeness every human being is made. It must include also "the preaching of the mystery of evil and, of the active pursuit of good . . . of the search for God first through prayer" and also through active membership of the Church including the reception of the sacraments.[269]

Furthermore, a very important task of proclamation is constantly to relate the gospel to the actual situation of the people or their lives. It must therefore include an explicit or clear message, adapted to the various conditions of life and continually updated, "concerning the rights and duties of the individual person and concerning family life, without which progress in the life of the individual is hardly possible." It has to deal also with the community life, with peace, justice, progress and the life of all nations. In addition, it must have a message about liberation, a message that is important and especially relevant for our time.[270]

Here the discussion on relating the gospel to the actual situation is based on the conviction that proclamation must be seen as relevant and possible in concrete human situations, both personal and social. The relationship here has three dimensions: anthropological, theological and evangelical. The anthropological relationship arises from the fact that the people to whom the gospel is to be preached are real human persons who are surely influenced by economic and social factors. The theological relationship has its origin in the close link between the plan of creation and that of redemption. For the fulfillment of earthly realities can be achieved only through the mystery of redemption "which extends to the very practical question of eradicating injustice and establishing justice." The evangelical link or relationship is rooted in Christian charity which is double-edged: love of God and love of neighbor. For there is no true love of God without love for neighbor, and there is no true love of neighbor without justice and peace. Hence it would be impossible to preach the gospel without true liberation and human development. [271]

Taking this three-fold relationship into consideration, the Church gives special preference to the poor in its missionary activity. For it wishes to restore the image or likeness of God in these human beings, an "image that has been obscured or even violated" by their lowly condition. It calls upon all Christians to align themselves with the poor and give them preferential attention; it considers this as a sure sign that the mission is that of Jesus Christ. Hence the Church showers praises and thanks on the missionaries who work in different ways to promote human advancement and to alleviate the sufferings of the poor. It gives support and guidelines to these missionaries.[272]

But it points out that the liberation that it preaches has its origin in God, not in socio-economic ideologies or political parties, which have "anthropocentric" goals or goals whose main aim is material progress. The object of proclamation cannot be reduced to such man-centered goals; if it were to be, proclamation would be merely earth-bound and lose its transcendent force. The liberation that the

Church preaches must embrace the whole human person, not just some spheres or parts of him. It cannot be restricted to any confined or limited sphere, be it social, economic, political or doctrinal. It has rather to embrace the whole human person in all aspects of man, extending even to his relationship with God. It is based on the proper understanding of the human person, "on a definite anthropology which can never be sacrificed for any reasons of strategy or custom or to achieve some transient success."[273]

This liberation which is concerned with the whole human person must have salvation in Christ at its center. (And any form of liberation that excludes this is earth-bound and quite defective.) To achieve this liberation which is integral, transcendent and yet promotes human advancement, the Church does not want the use of any form of violence, but rather advocates the conversion of consciences through evangelization. For through the conversion of the heart and people's ways of thinking, evangelization helps them to recognize each person's dignity, fosters commitment, solidarity, and service to the neighbor. It thus gives every person a place in the divine economy: the building of the kingdom of God, a kingdom of peace and justice, beginning already here on earth. [274]

The Means of Proclamation

There are two main means of contact in proclamation. The Church rightly observes that today there are means of social communication or mass media (the press, the radio, the television, the video or movie, the computer and others) which can reach and influence many people.[275] It therefore urges all members of the Church to work together to "ensure that the means of communication are put at the service of the multiple forms of the apostolate without delay".[276] Christians, it says, should have themselves to blame, if only owing to the high costs involved in possessing and running these media or for any other reason, they fail to use them to spread the gospel message.[277] It stresses the point that Christ's command to his Church to carry the good news to every part of the world should not be regarded as being fully obeyed until all available means of communication have been adequately employed in this regard. Christians therefore will feel guilty before God if they do not make good use of these instruments for apostolic work or rather the proclamation of the gospel. [278]

But the mass media are not the substitute for personal contact which has been the general and most common method of contact in evangelization from apostolic times to the present. Through this means the conscience of an individual can be touched by some inspiring word or testimony from a Christian.[279] All Christians, both clergy and laity alike, are urged not to belittle this method which is almost always available, but rather to use it whenever necessary.[280]

(iii) Inculturation or Incarnation of the Gospel in People's Cultures

We noted at the beginning of this chapter that the aim of evangelization is conversion: conversion of individual and collective consciences, people's way of thinking and acting, and the whole environment in which they live. This cannot be done effectively if the gospel does not impregnate the culture of the people, since it is culture that makes people who they are; it determines their world-view and mentality and by it the people are identified. People evangelized without proper inculturation usually have superficial faith because the gospel has not deeply influenced the culture; for, just as food is to human life so culture is to the life of a community. And it must be pointed out here that evangelization of the culture or inculturation is not mere adaptation of the gospel to the culture. For adaptation is only accommodation or adjustment introduced into a given dominant format or structure; the structure itself remains unchanged. An example of adaptation in the liturgy includes the use of the vernacular and indigenous symbols in the rites while the formats of the rites remain unchanged. With regard to a given culture, for instance, the Igbo culture, the adaptation approach would leave unchanged the format of the Mass, for example, while using the Igbo language and musical instruments during the celebration.[281] But "inculturation is different from a simple external adaptation because it means the intimate transformation of authentic cultural values through their integration in Christianity in the various human cultures."[282]

The classical example of inculturation in evangelization is the case of Father Matteo Ricci and the Chinese rite. Because of the marvelous results Ricci's inculturation achieved and the disastrous consequences that followed when this was misunderstood and forbidden, we shall consider it here as an example of both the marvels inculturation can bring about and the great harm that can be done to evangelization when it is belittled or rejected.

Father Matteo Ricci, a Jesuit priest from Macereta, Italy arrived in China in 1582. At that period the Chinese life was totally permeated by Confucian cultural values. Among these values was the virtue of filial piety which became elaborated in the extraordinary reverence shown to ancestors. During the funeral of a member of a family a paper object with the deceased's name written on it was placed before the corpse and accompanied the corpse to the grave site. After burial it was returned to the home and placed on a small altar where it received the homage of the mourners. Eventually it was replaced by what was called the 'spirit tablet', usually made of wood, which bore the name of the deceased, the family status, and rank in society. On its back was written the date of birth and death of the deceased. This memorial tablet in some sense represented the personality of the deceased and carried the inscription *shen wei,* that is, 'the seat of the spirit' of the deceased.

The members of the family, who assembled before the domestic shrine, believed that the souls of the departed were in some way present in the tablets. Hence the mourners made various gestures of respect or reverence before them. They bowed and knelt before lighted candles, and burnt incense and paper money before the memorial tablets. On certain fixed occasions, such as the anniversary of the death of the departed or on the fifteenth day of the Chinese month, members of the family held a meeting before the shrine where they made offerings of food and drink placing these items in front of the shrine. Later they partook of these offerings in a common banquet.[283]

Ricci and other missionaries were faced with serious questions. Were the ancestral rites to be understood as a form of religious worship or rather as a form of reverence to the dead, similar to the practice in Europe of placing flowers on the tombstones, praying for the dead and displaying their pictures as forms of memorial or love for them? This and similar questions were not easy for Europeans to answer. With his profound knowledge of Chinese culture and life, Ricci, however, quickly realized that the family was the key to the Chinese social system and the funeral rites together with the ancestral rites made up the social constitution that supported the system itself. He therefore concluded that the ancestral rites were not religious worship but rather reverence for the dead. Chinese who became Christian could continue to practice them. Ricci, the apostle of China saw them as agreeing with or similar to the Catholic belief in the immortality of the soul.

Thanks to his mastery of the Chinese culture including the language, literature and antiquities, Ricci was able to evangelize not only individuals but also their culture. Many Chinese were converted not only because they discovered in their ancient books the fundamental doctrine which the missionaries proclaimed but also especially because of the incarnational approach of Father Ricci. He won the hearts of many Chinese including the emperor. When he died in 1610 he was mourned by thousands of Christians who were the fruits of his labors. [284]

Some twenty years later, however, other missionaries from other religious congregations, notably the Dominicans, began arriving in China. Not endowed with the prudence and sensitivity of Ricci, they saw the Chinese rites as idolatry and reported this to Rome, thereby setting off a controversy over the Chinese rites. The controversy involved several popes and lasted for a whole century, from 1643 to

1742. When in 1742 Rome issued a decree condemning the Chinese rites, the controversy was ended and ended also in consequence was the European mission in China. For the Chinese became very angry and determined to prohibit a religion that was clearly opposed to their fundamental customs. And in the nineteenth century, when Catholic missionaries resumed activities in China, they were viewed with suspicion and associated with European colonial expansionism. Although several popes in succeeding generations have made overtures of goodwill toward China (including the termination by Pope Pius XII in December 1939 of the prohibition of the Chinese rites), the Church and its missionaries have not come close to the progress made by Father Matteo Ricci there four centuries ago. [285]

Later generations have come to appreciate the wisdom and foresight of Ricci. For instance speaking on October 25, 1982, the fourth centenary of the arrival of Father Ricci in China, Pope John Paul II showered praises on the missionary from Macereta. He observed that it was owing to "the work of inculturation that Father Ricci . . . succeeded in carrying out a work which seemed impossible." He urges other missionaries to imitate this example.[286]

The case of Chinese rites illustrates that inculturation is the challenging or transforming of a culture from within. Christ and his message challenge a culture without altering its essential character or destroying it. He succeeds in this because he challenges a culture from within, not from without. He was so identified with his own culture that his contemporaries failed to recognize him as God. It was owing to his being a perfect Jew that he succeeded in challenging the Jewish culture. After his resurrection he and his message similarly challenge every culture from within.[287] It is only where the gospel and the culture are properly married that the Church can appear to non-Christians and Christian neophytes as a palpable form of Christ's saving grace.[288] Hence the Church especially since the Second Vatican Council insistently directs that the culture of the convert or prospective convert must be evangelized. The council urges missionaries and Christians living among non-Christians to use "the customs, traditions, wisdom, teaching, arts and sciences of their people" to glorify God and spread the good news.[289] And it makes it clear that "there are many links between the message of salvation and culture." For God in revealing himself to man in the past, the revelation which culminated in the incarnation, spoke according to the culture proper to each age, and continues to speak today to every people according to its culture. The Church which is sent to every age and nation is not indissolubly tied or bound to "any race or nation, to any one particular way of life, or to any customary practices, ancient or modern." It should therefore enter into true marriage with every culture anywhere in the world.[290]

These statements of the Second Vatican Council can be regarded as hints or indications of the direction the Church wishes to go to with regard to culture. *Evangelii Nuntiandi* published ten years after the council is more specific. It emphasizes the importance of inculturation and states its limits. It points out that the Church has to transmit "whole and entire" to the world its heritage of truth and "at the same time seek to present this heritage to the men of our time in a form which is at once clear and convincing."[291] The document goes on to confirm what we have indicated before; that is, that inculturation, unlike mere adaptation of the gospel to the environment, is not something external but rather a real permeation, indeed a real incarnation of the gospel where it finds itself. "The gospel must impregnate the culture and the whole way of life of man," the human person and his relationship with God thus being at the center. The document goes further to make it clear that Christianity is not a culture and that the gospel cannot be identified with any particular culture. Both Christianity and the gospel transcend every culture. Both too can penetrate, endorse or challenge any culture for the building up of the kingdom of God and the well-being of the human beings who live in the culture. The document laments the rift between the gospel and human cultures and exhorts Christians to see that the rift is removed by having these cultures evangelized or penetrated by the gospel.[292]

Pope John Paul II has continued the teaching of *Evangelii Nuntiandi* and in many addresses during his various travels around the world he zealously spreads the message of inculturation which he sees as an expression of the incarnation. Speaking, for instance, to the bishops of Zaire or Congo on May 3, 1980, he said, "One aspect of evangelization is inculturation of the gospel or the Africanization of the Church . . . . It is part of the effort we must make to incarnate the message of Christ."[293] And at his meeting with Nigerian bishops in Lagos in February 1982, he reminded them that the "whole dimension of the inculturation of the gospel into the lives of your people" was an important aspect of the evangelizing role of the bishops. He pointed out that it is through God's providence that the message of salvation is made incarnate and is "communicated through the culture of each people." The path of culture, he maintained, is the path of man, and that it is on that path that man encounters God who reveals himself to each people through its own culture. The pontiff made it clear that "the gospel of Christ, the incarnate Word, finds its home along the path of culture and from this path it continues to offer its message of salvation and eternal life."[294]

In his encyclical *Redemptoris Missio* he expresses the urgency of inculturation in evangelization, pointing out the dialectical interaction between the Church and culture in this process. For through inculturation the Church makes the gospel message incarnate in different cultures while at the same time it introduces the different peoples as well as their cultures into its own community. And hence "through inculturation the Church for her part becomes a more intelligible sign of what she is and a more effective instrument of mission." The pontiff admonishes missionaries working in foreign lands to "immerse themselves in the cultural milieu" of the people among whom they are working, learn their language, and become familiar with the cultural expressions and values. Only in this way will they succeed in bringing to the people "the knowledge of the hidden mystery . . . in a credible and fruitful way."[295]

We see thus the emphasis the Church lays on inculturation. This is understandable. For the Church as a sacrament or saving sign must appear thus to every people in the way they can understand, in an intelligible manner. And there is no other way it can do this apart from involving itself and the gospel message in the people's way of life, that is to say, their culture. One point the Church stresses often is that the gospel message and the Christian religion cannot be subservient to any culture. They are open to every culture but cannot be dominated by any. When the Christian message comes to any culture, it comes as a double-edged sword: to endorse and to challenge its views and values. It must find something to agree with and something to disagree with. It confirms the agreeable values and endeavors to purify what needs to be purified. It is when a culture has thus been purified and permeated by the Christian message that that culture and its society can be considered evangelized.[296] Hence the Church expresses the urgency of inculturation or the evangelization of culture.

Proclamation and Religious Liberty

Before we leave this chapter we have to touch briefly the Church's stand on religious liberty. The Second Vatican Council gave one full document, *Dignitatis Humanae* or *Declaration on Religious Liberty* to this subject. The document states that God has revealed to the world that salvation for mankind is to be found only in Christ. Because the Church is seen as the historical continuation of Christ's presence in the world and has his mandate to carry on missionary activity, *Dignitatis Humanae* maintains that the "one true religion continues to exist in the Catholic and Apostolic Church, to which the Lord Jesus entrusted the task of spreading . . . among all men" the good news of salvation in Christ. And every person, it says, is bound in conscience to seek the truth, especially the truth about God and his Church and to accept and retain it once it is found. Therefore, the Second Vatican Council's teaching on religious freedom first of all demands that freedom which human beings need to fulfill their obligation to worship God. This means "freedom from coercion in civil society", while "it leaves intact the traditional Catholic teaching on the moral duty of individuals and societies toward the true religion and the one Church of Christ."[297]

Furthermore, the document recognizes the dignity of the human person endowed with a conscience, which is his private and innermost sanctuary, where he himself has to make the decisions concerning his last end. Hence it insists that no human authority should violate this sanctuary, the human conscience, which every person is bound to follow "faithfully in all his activity so that he can come to God", his last end. This means no one must be forced to act contrary to his conscience, nor yet "be prevented from acting according to his conscience, especially in religious matters."[298]

Thus recognizing the dignity of the human person and following the example of Christ and the apostles, the Church shows respect for every person's conscience. Therefore, no one is to be coerced or forced into believing for whatever reason. But this is different, with all due respect, from challenging people's consciences with the good news of the kingdom of God. That is to say, forcing or coercing into believing is not the same thing as presenting clearly and convincingly to non-Christians and others the message of salvation in Christ, and leaving them free to make their decision to accept or reject it. The Church says that it and its members are bound to do the latter, to present the message of salvation to others. It reiterates the duty imposed on it by Christ, its master and founder, to spread the good news to the whole world and make disciples of all nations. No effort should be spared in fulfilling this command.[299] In a word, therefore, the position of the Church on religious liberty in relation to proclamation is that the Church and its members are bound to use every available legitimate means to spread the good news to the whole world. But nobody should be in any way coerced into believing or accepting the gospel message.

CHAPTER EIGHT

TOWARD BETTER RELATIONS AND PROCLAMATION

It should be clear by now that the Catholic Church takes both inter-religious dialogue and the proclamation of the gospel seriously. Both are seen as important aspects of its mission. In this chapter we shall consider how this two-pronged task can be undertaken even more successfully. In the course of this book we have noted the efforts of the Catholic Church to promote dialogue or good relations with non-Christian religions. These efforts have a lot of challenges as we noted in previous chapters. Thus dialogue is a very demanding task which requires patience, humility and genuine love. Much has been achieved. Yet much more needs to be done to improve these relations. We have noted also that while the Church admits the possibility of salvation in these religions it sees the need to proclaim the good news of Jesus Christ to them. In addition to what has been discussed before, we shall make some suggestions as to the way to undertake simultaneously inter-religious dialogue and proclamation of the good news. These suggestions, I hope, can make the relations between Christians and their non-Christian neighbors even better and promote the cause of proclamation.

For Better Relations

A few suggestions will first be made here to help make even better the good relations of the Church with non-Christian religions. These are suggestions as to what both sides of the dialogue are to do to promote better relations. And since the Church is in the forefront of the crusade to promote good relations with non-Christian religions, it is expected to take the lead in implementing these suggestions. Before we begin, however, it is good to remember, as we have seen before, that the Church faces more and greater challenges in its dialogue with Islam, probably the second largest world religion after the Christian religion. Though the suggestions may apply in the dialogue with all non-Christian religions, they apply more in the Church's relations with Islam.

Healing the Past

The history of the relations between the Church and some non-Christian religions is full of sad memories or hostilities. In order to heal these sad memories it is necessary for both Christians and the different non-Christian religions concerned to study with sincerity their history. Wrongs committed in the past should be acknowledged. Pardon should be sought and given. This will open the door for reconciliation and better understanding. Commendation or praise should be given too to the religions that have made reasonable contributions to the betterment of culture, science, and human development in general.[300]

And while studying the past to improve the future, Christians and non-Christians should endeavor to learn the unpleasant exercise of self-examination or self-criticism. Pope John Paul II, in preparation for the third millennium, calls on the Catholic Church to examine its past and recall the times in the past when Christians failed to live according to the spirit of Christ and his Gospel but rather "indulged in ways of thinking and acting which were truly forms of counter-witness and scandal." The pontiff points out that though the Church is holy, it acknowledges as its own sinful men and women in its ranks and files. He urges Christians all over the world, "to purify themselves, through repentance, of past errors and instances of infidelity, inconsistency, and slowness to act."[301]

On March 12, 2000, the first Sunday of Lent, the same pope himself took the initiative to publicly ask pardon for the sins of Christians through the ages. The sins that he asked pardon for included "sins against Christian unity, the use of violence in serving the truth, hostility toward the Jews and other religions, marginalization of women, and wrongs—like abortion—against society's weakest members." To make it clear that he was apologizing on behalf of all Christians he added, "For the part that each of us, with his behavior, has had in these evils that have disfigured the face of the Church, we humbly ask forgiveness." At the end of the Mass he promised that such sins would never be committed again.[302] In different parts of the Catholic world many bishops followed the pope's example and apologized for the sins of Christians through the ages in their areas of jurisdiction. For instance, in Boston, Cardinal Bernard Law, on behalf of Christians, asked for forgiveness for sins regarding anti-Semitism, slavery, racism, etc. Australian bishops apologized for their failures in dealing with Church unity, etc.; and Swiss bishops acknowledged that Catholics did too little to prevent the persecution of the Jews by the Nazis.[303] And on his pilgrimage and visit to the Holy Land, the pope, on 23 March 2000, at the Holocaust Memorial center, apologized specifically for the persecution of the Jews by Christians in history. He stated: "I assure the Jewish people that the Catholic Church, motivated by the gospel law of truth and love and by no political considerations, is deeply saddened by the hatred, acts of persecution and displays of anti-Semitism directed against the Jews by Christians at any time and in any place."[304] If non-Christian religions will also examine their own collective conscience and call on all their members to seek repentance in their own past wrongs, it will help to make the relations between them and Christians even better.

Promotion of Religious Freedom

Christians and non-Christians must realize that religious pluralism is a reality of our time. Thanks especially to progress in communication, transportation, business and technology, we now live in a pluralistic world. Our world is in fact now regarded as a global village where in many places Christians and non-Christians live or work as neighbors. They both therefore must learn to live and let live. While adherents of any side take interest in their own religion they must know also that others have love for their own too. Force in any form should not be used to make other people change their religion. Religious freedom based on respect for the human person and in accordance with the United Nations charter on human rights should be accorded to all, individuals and communities. The Catholic Church today allows freedom of worship to members of all religions. For instance, on June 21, 1995 the first mosque was inaugurated in Rome, the capital or center of Christianity. The Church did not oppose that project or work against it.[305] But is it possible today for the Catholic Church to inaugurate openly a church in a world-wide center of a non-Christian religion, say, Mecca or anywhere in Saudi Arabia? The Church's goodwill should also meet goodwill from other religions, if dialogue is to make real progress. The desire to improve the relations must be the concern of all the religions not just of one religion or a few. Fanaticism in all its forms must be avoided. Religious fanatics in different religions need to undergo a real conversion. For anyone who uses force to make another change his religion does not know the merciful and kind God who has made all human beings in his image and likeness and has endowed them with freewill and conscience. Religious leaders have the duty then, especially today, to train the adherents of their religions to learn to be tolerant and to live peaceably with people of other faiths.

Another important task of religious leaders is to endeavor to separate religion from politics. This may not be an easy undertaking since in some religions, notably Islam, as was indicated earlier, religion and politics are closely intertwined. When a religion is thus too closely associated with or married to politics, it will surely share in the blame resulting from the mistakes or excesses of politicians. Moreover, that close intimacy may lead some over-zealous politicians to use their political power to unduly influence people of other faiths to become members of their own religions.

Dialogue To Be Based on Deep Religious Experience

Religious dialogue is very important and must be engaged in not only by academic experts but also and especially by people who are deeply religious—people who have had real deep religious experience and are aware of the omnipresence of God. This does not mean the exclusion of academic experts. What it does rather mean is that for inter-religious dialogue today to make real progress, most of those who take active part in the dialogue must be people who have deep spirituality in their own religious traditions and who listen to the Spirit of God continuously. They must be people who are open to truth no matter where it is found. In the actual dialogue or discussion each participant should not try to impose his own truth on others but must present his view patiently, clearly and respectfully. While holding to his own truth he has to presume, at least tentatively, that the position of other participant is also true. This means he should listen with genuine interest and sympathy; he should endeavor to see the truth also from the other participant's point of view and submit to that truth when he is convinced of it. He should be ready to change or even perhaps abandon his beliefs or certain beliefs of his own religion when this becomes necessary. Therefore, dialogue is not possible if the participants enter it with the supposition that they alone possess the final, irreformable truth, and are resolved even beforehand never to make any concessions. For progress to be made the participants must be ready to make necessary concessions provided this does no harm to their own religious traditions.

Working Together on Common Projects

Working together on projects of common interest can help also to promote inter-religious harmony: projects aimed at alleviating human suffering. Such are projects to check or minimize the effects of natural disasters including earthquakes, floods, erosion and hurricanes. Different religions can also present a common front against the imbalance in the distribution of the world's resources, God's provision for all his children on earth. For it has been noted that only twenty percent of the people on earth consume eighty percent of the earth's resources.[306] This can be prevented by different religions working together.

Dialogue of Life and Faith

In addition to the suggestions made above, the dialogue of life and faith, which was mentioned in chapter one, can be very helpful in promoting harmonious co-existence between Christians and non-Christians, especially in places where there are continual conflicts between Christians and their non-Christian neighbors. This plan is already working in some places, for example in Marawi, the Philippines, where Christians and Moslems are living together. Any religious tradition can use this plan. But in making the suggestions in these pages we have the Catholic Church especially in mind. This aspect of dialogue has three spheres or rather moments, namely, articulation, organization, and immersion.

(i) *Articulation*. The diocese or Catholic body that wishes to introduce this type of dialogue has to do some homework beforehand. This should include finding out why Christians and non-Christians of the area come into conflict with each other; inquiring whether the government can offer any help; enlisting the help of some priest or some other Christian who has some knowledge of the religion and culture of the non-Christian neighbors. The aim is to evolve a well-articulated vision of the program of action. To obtain help for this, the diocese should sponsor a workshop on inter-religious dialogue. The participants, who should represent at least a cross section of the diocese, priests, religious, and laity, should be asked to write down their ideas, feelings, experiences and dreams about dialogue with the non-Christian neighbors. These ideas should be collected and a plan of the vision of dialogue drawn from them. This plan may require revision later. [307]

(ii) *Organization*. The diocese's aim here should be to form a group of Christians whose main purpose is dialogue with non-Christians. The main activities therefore at the early stage should be directed toward the Christian community, to prepare Christians for dialogue. About one year is devoted to retreats and seminars which should be designed to help Christians to discover their prejudices and acquire what is needed to cope with or extirpate them. Care should be taken to note the participants who show some signs of openness. These should be invited to take part in future meetings which will help them to form themselves and others for dialogue of faith and life.

The actual dialogue should begin with the young or the youth in the school, college or university setting. During the week a specific time should be set aside for conversation between Christians and non-Christians, teachers as well as students. The topic for discussion should come from both the Christian and non-Christian participants. The aim will be to enable Christians and their non-Christian neighbors to share what is good in Christianity and also in the non-Christian religion, Islam for example. To avoid the session being misunderstood, it should not be called dialogue; some other name such as "current affairs" or "harmony" could be used. In a college or university setting there should be a group of Christian students whose objective should be to have contacts with and befriend non-Christian students. Non-Christian students thus befriended should be introduced to the Christian chaplaincy of the college or university which should keep the contact or friendship alive. Plans should be made for the Christian group to study about once a week the tenets of the non-Christian religion in question and also the culture of the members of that religion, if this is different from that of their Christian neighbors.

The diocese will help to promote the dialogue if it allows Christians, as much as this is possible, to observe some feasts of the non-Christian religion, for instance the Moslem feast of Ramadan. And the diocese or parish could give to the non-Christians, who show more openness and interest, occasions to interact and work with Christians. This could be done by inviting them to speak on dialogue in gatherings of Christians; or to be part of what may be called an awareness committee which should, among other things, collect information on injustices being done to anyone, Christian or non-Christian; the purpose of this being to find out the sources of conflict in order to uproot them. There also should be some time, such as the occasion of a Christian or non-Christian feast, when the Christians and non-Christians should meditate together and pray-according to their beliefs. Apart from this, constant appeals should be made to Christians to pray for the success of the dialogue in the diocese or parish.[308]

(iii) *Immersion*. What has been said so far in this section of the chapter is for the preparation of the Christian community. Where possible, there should be a number of strong Christians who can live among the non-Christians, not to convert them, hut simply to be there with them bearing silent witness thereby unobtrusively bridging the gap of misunderstanding. This has been done successfully in the Philippines. There some priests and religious brothers live in small huts in the Moslem towns. In one other town a priest spends his afternoon with Christians, but his morning hours he usually spends in a Moslem store as an attendant. This helps him to meet with many of the Moslems and to learn their culture. In Bangladesh where eighty-eight percent of the population are Moslems, eleven percent Hindus and less than a half percent Christians, A Maryknoll priest, Father Robert McCahill practices also this type of dialogue of faith and life. Since twenty-four years he has chosen to live in rural towns of this south-east Asian nation. He stays three years in one place before moving to another, in each case living in a tiny hut. From his hut he takes off early in the morning riding his bicycle around the neighborhood, as it were, seeking people to help. Usually as he rides along, he is stopped by relatives or neighbors of the sick who need to be taken to hospital and cared for. The priest does this work with disinterested love, without even trying to convert the people to Christianity. The first usual reaction or feeling of the people toward him is that of suspicion. But by the third year of his stay their sentiments change to trust and sincere affection. His activities have not only won him love among the people, they have also helped to bridge the relationship between Christians and their non-Christian neighbors there.[309] This aspect of dialogue, the aspect of thus living among non-Christians, is called "immersion." Simple Christians living or working among non-Christians can apply "immersion". They can do this by showing sincere interest or love to the non-Christian neighbors, without introducing religion too early.[310]

Furthermore, it is important that courses relating to inter-religious dialogue be taught in seminaries throughout the Catholic world, so that future priests may learn not only how to evangelize but also how to enter into genuine dialogue with non-Christians. There should be seminars and workshops about non-Christian religions even among Christians who are not actually living among or working with non-Christians. This prepares the Christian for any future encounter with non-Christians. Fanaticism, as said earlier, should be condemned and uprooted. And here it may be added that it is important to develop properly or clearly the Christian theology of non-Christian religions and of dialogue too. This will help to provide guidelines in the actual practice of dialogue.

As indicated above, these suggestions are made for any religion, Christian or non-Christian, which sincerely desires dialogue. The, Catholic Church is here only used as an example of how a religious body can use the suggestions, and because the Church has been in the vanguard of inter-religious dialogue. For dialogue to be meaningful and balanced, however, all sides must be ready to make their own contribution toward harmony.

The Place of Proclamation

But the Church's undertaking is not dialogue alone. She insists also on the proclamation of the good news. The Christian's love for his non-Christian neighbors is not genuine if, all things being equal, he stops at only dialogue. He should do all he can to see the good relationship continue to grow. He should not only love the non-Christian neighbors; he should love also what they love which is not incompatible with the Christian religion. When this relationship of friendship and trust has been established, and circumstances permitting, the Christian should also introduce the good news. Let us take, for instance a Christian missionary nurse working in a non-Christian environment. The first thing she should do is to show the patients and other non-Christians that she loves them; that they are important to her and that she is happy to work among them. She would not need to say this explicitly. But if she wants to reach the people she must act this out in what she does. She should show personal interest in each of the patients. This interest should extend to their language, the culture of their people, their interests and tears, their joys and sorrows. Then at a favorable time she should introduce the good news to her patients and others. Her first attempt may not be successful but that is no reason for her to lose heart. She must not, however, for any reason try to impose the message on anyone. Nor should she bribe people into believing by, for instance, promising to pay the hospital bills of the poor patients who have no insurance, if they agree to become Christians.[311] This would be contrary to the Church's teaching. The good news and conversion are gifts from God and should not be imposed or otherwise cheapened by a sort of bribery. The Church simply wants the gospel message to be presented as clearly as possible after necessary obstacles have been cleared. Those who hear the message are left free to make their choice to become Christians or not. The clearing of obstacles on their way is best done by witness, inculturation and other ways of establishing friendship and trust.

Some scholars are of a different view, however; they see the Church's missionary task in a different light. According to them conversion is no longer required today. For them the Church's missionary activity should now be modified in such a way that the presence of the Church or missionaries will have to act only as a catalyst. And by this they mean that no attempt should be made to convert non-Christians or make them join the Church; missionaries or the representatives of the Church should be available mainly for dialogue with non-Christians and to help their religions to improve themselves, to bring out the best in them. This view is sometimes so nuanced that it assigns a merely sign function to the Church or concedes that the Church should proclaim the good news but should not necessarily seek conversion: its main mission is to represent the love of God, to give witness to hope and to be a sign of hope in the world.[312]

This, certainly, is not the position of the Catholic Church. As the sacrament or real symbol of Christ, the light of the world, the Church, by promoting dialogue or friendly relations with non-Christian religions (and other groups, including non-believers), wishes first of all to remind the world that all human beings are made in the image of God, who is also the origin and ultimate destiny of all. Hence it is setting an example to the world to opt for peaceful co-existence and co-operation and to use dialogue rather than violence in settling differences. It has never, however, abdicated its desire or rather mission to convert non-Christians. As has been indicated before, the Church makes it clear that the main aim of proclamation is conversion which includes entry into the Church. Until it succeeds in converting and bringing into the full communion of the Catholic Church those who hear the proclaiming of the good news, proclamation has not attained its main aim or fruit. It will be seen as attaining its goal when it leads those who hear the good news to accept it fully. This full acceptance of the message of salvation is expressed "by the visible and objective entry of a man into the community of the faithful . . . that community is the Church, the visible sacrament of salvation."[313] This entry into the Church will

131

prove its sincerity by certain signs that must be manifest. Among them are fidelity to the Church, frequent and worthy reception of the sacraments of the Church, and serious involvement in the Church's missionary activity in such a way that the evangelized becomes the evangelizer. [314]

What has been said in the preceding paragraph does not mean the denial of the possibility of salvation in non-Christian religions. These religious traditions have been the religions available to millions of different peoples for centuries, and they have helped their adherents to find solutions to a lot of life's problems or to cope with the challenges of the human condition. And they have served as vehicles of salvation to some of their adherents. As has been shown at different places in this book, especially in chapter one, the Church sees positive qualities or values in these religions. Yet it sees the need for Christian missionary activity in them to purify and restore in Christ the good elements found in them. "So whatever goodness is found" in them "far from being lost is purified, raised to a higher level and reaches its perfection, for the glory of God."[315] These religions are seen as related or oriented to the Church of Christ, who has a unique role in the coming of the kingdom of God. Part of the Church's mission is to recognize that the incipient "reality of this kingdom can be found also beyond the confines of the Church," in other religious traditions. But this is only an incipient reality which "needs to find completion through being related to the kingdom of Christ already present in the Church yet only realized fully in the world to come."[316]

Thus the Church rejects the idea of equating it with other religions. Speaking at the plenary meeting of the Congregation for the Doctrine of the Faith on January 28, 2000, Pope John Paul II condemned the liberal mentality which tends to relativize Christ and the Church. He warned that if this mentality is permitted to continue it would make the Church lose its reason for existence. He pointed out that the uniqueness of the Church has its basis in "the salvific mediation of Christ." Jesus himself founded this Church "as a salvific reality: as his body, through which he himself operates in the history of salvation." And just as there is one Christ, there is only one body of Christ: "only one Catholic and Apostolic Church." He saw as erroneous the idea that the Church is "a way of salvation equal to those of other religions," or the mentality which holds that one religion is as good as the other. The pontiff restated the Second Vatican Council's teaching on the possibility of salvation for non-Christians. He, however, made it clear that "they find themselves in a deficient situation, compared to those who have the fullness of salvific means in the Church."[317] The pope's teaching was taken up later in the year by the Congregation of the Doctrine of the Faith, which presented it as a doctrine in a document called *Declaration "Dominus Jesus."*[318]

The last point made by the pope needs to be stressed. Non-Christian religions may be helpful to their adherents; but they can never be comparable to the Church as a way of salvation. They are to be commended in so far as they are different human responses to the same divine reality or God, and in so far as they can be vehicles of saving grace to some of their adherents. But they far fall short of the riches of Christianity. The uniqueness of Christianity lies in the incarnation of the Word, in God becoming man. In this religion it is no longer the case of man searching for God, but rather of "God who comes in Person to speak to man of himself and to show him the path by which he may be reached." In this case it is no longer man's blind search for God, but rather the response of faith to God who himself searches for man (as the incarnation of the Word attests) and reveals himself.[319] And as we noted before, by his incarnation or becoming man, Jesus Christ bridged the chasm between God and man, becoming the personification of God's reaching out to mankind and mankind's response to God's offer. In him all creation responds to God. He is "thus the fulfillment of the yearning of all the world's religions and, as such, he is their sole and definitive completion."[320]

In concluding this chapter, I wish to sum up very briefly some of the most important points we have covered in this book so far. From the Second Vatican Council to the present, the Catholic Church seeks or promotes friendly relations with non-Christian religions. Various factors helped the Church to adopt this positive attitude toward these religions. The three most important of them are: first, the realization that non-Christians make up the majority of the world population; second, the fact that Christians today inevitably have to live and work together with non-Christians and hence the need for inter-religious harmony; third, the pastoral influence of the Second Vatican Council. This council enabled the Church to have a better understanding of the unity of the human race; that all human beings created in the image or likeness of God have one and the same origin and destiny: God. It was especially this understanding that made the Church resolve to seek and promote friendly relations or dialogue with non-Christian religions.

The Church has taken this dialogue very seriously. Among its various efforts to promote the friendly relations is the creation of a number of institutions for dialogue. The two most important of these are the Commission for Religious Relations with the Jews, and the Secretariat (or Council) for Inter-religious Dialogue. The former officially represents the Church in its relations with the Jews and

Judaism; the latter is concerned with the Church's official dialogue with all other non-Christian religions. In addition to all these, the popes, especially Pope John Paul II, through their visits and meetings with non-Christian religious leaders, promote dialogue.

Thanks to this amicable attitude toward non-Christian religious, the Catholic Church now sees some positive qualities in them and admits that the salvation won by Christ is possible to non-Christians, not only as individuals but even through the positive qualities of their religions. In these religions can be found the incipient reality of the kingdom of God. This incipient reality has, however, to find its completion in the Church, though the total fulfillment will be in the hereafter. Hence, the Catholic Church, as the historical continuation of Christ, who has a unique role in the coming of this kingdom, has to proclaim the gospel message to non-Christians to enable them to come into the Church in which the incipient reality of the kingdom found in their religions has its completion. It is the one religion which has the fullness of the means of salvation, because it is the sacrament of Christ, the savior of the world. Moreover, as such a sacrament, it has to appear palpably as a saving sign everywhere in the world. This necessarily implies that it has to proclaim the gospel everywhere and to all who have not heard it. This duty is made even more binding by the fact that Christ, its founder and master, commanded the Church to do so. Because of these reasons, the Church sees the proclamation of the gospel not as an option, but as a duty given to it by God. It therefore warns Christians that their own salvation may be placed in jeopardy if they do not take seriously God's commission to them to proclaim the good news. It puts it this way: "If, however, through lack of zeal or lack of courage, . . . or in deference to false theories, we fail to proclaim the gospel, can we ourselves be saved?"[321]

We can see from this book that the Catholic Church does not deny the possibility of salvation in non-Christian religions. It however insists on the proclamation of the gospel to non-Christians. Why? Because the Church is the ordinary or usual way of salvation as planned by God himself. All things being equal, therefore, a Christian has a far better chance of being saved than a non-Christian. Thus dialogue and the proclamation of the gospel are both important to the Church. It wants all Christians to be personally seriously involved in both. 1 hope the careful reading of the book will help to dispel the confusion which has ensued in some quarters in connection with dialogue and proclamation since the Church began to undertake both seriously.

CHAPTER NINE

BEYOND DIALOGUE: THE CHALLENGE OF SECULARISM, CULTS AND SECTS

The Church is insistent on the necessity of proclamation in non-Christian religions. This is good and a sign of the Church's love for the adherents of these religions. But what about other groups that Christians seem to lose sight of, groups that are neither Christian nor do they belong properly to the non-Christian world religions that we know? I mean the groups that sometimes pose problems or rather challenges not only for proclamation and inter-religious dialogue but even for society as a whole. Included in these groups are mainly those who embrace secularism and pseudo-religious movements. Is it not time that Christians paid more attention to them? While not abandoning evangelizing or proclaiming the good news in non-Christian religions, much more attention should be given to secularism and these pseudo-religious movements as well as the threat they pose not only to the Christian religion but to society as a whole.

Secularism is a dangerous phenomenon. A society where many people do not believe in God or have no sense of the supernatural is simply not easy to live in; it is indeed a horrifying society. Unfortunately this canker is fast spreading in our world. In the United States, for example, it has been noted that eighty million people have no religious family to which they are actively affiliated.[322] And according to a survey, only eighteen percent of the population of Britain describes itself as Christian. The neighboring France, once described as "the eldest daughter of the Church," does not fare better.[323]

This is a clear sign that secularism is widespread in the world today and this does not augur well for society. Why? Because secularism usually brings in its train dangerous consequences. Among these is resort to occultism. For, man is created to worship a higher power, God. If he fails to do this, idols of different kinds force themselves on him. This is one of the reasons some people sometimes resort to magic and other forms of occultism. Lamentably many young people are falling prey to this disease and its dangerous aftermath. An example is the case of a fourteen-year old eighth-grader, Thomas Sullivan, Jr. of Sparta, New Jersey. In early January 1988, Sullivan, who was not strongly committed to any religion, had lately got himself deeply involved with Satanism by reading books on devils in an attempt to get a good grade in a class project. This made him begin to suffer demonic molestations. These included bizarre actions that could not be explained otherwise. The family members and the boy's friends observed the sudden change in him. No psychologist or psychiatrist could help. The family knew the boy needed spiritual help but did not know where to get such help. Greater disaster followed. A newspaper summarized what happened with the following statement: "A 'B' mark on religion class assignment set off a bizarre series of events, including Satanic worship, that culminated Saturday in a fourteen-year old eighth-grader stabbing his mother to death, setting his house afire, and cutting his own throat with his Boys' Scout knife."[324] This is only one example of the horrors that secularism and its concomitants are bringing to families and society every day.

Satan worship or Satanism has different forms and shades; and it is often sugar-coated with some apparently attractive doctrines and features which can lure the young to its trap. One of the most dangerous forms is the New Age, which teaches its adherents that their inner self is God. They have, therefore, to do for themselves whatever people believe God can do for them; they have to create whatever they want: health, illness, happiness, affluence, rain, sunshine, etc.[325] This form of Satanism is a blend of social, spiritual, and political forces and includes in its program sociology, theology, medicine, anthropology, the physical sciences, history, the human potential movement, sports, and science fiction. It is a sort of pantheism which attempts to deify everything existing.[326] Enjoying massive support from the social media in the United States, especially through children's video and cartoons, it is now attracting a very large following. [327]

Observant pastors, however, are becoming aware of the dangers the New Age and other forms of Satanism pose for society and the speed with which they are spreading. These pastors sometimes point out the factors or actions that promote this nefarious involvement. When on March 4, 1990, Cardinal John O'Connor of New York spoke out against "rock music" as an aid to Satan worship, he was only pointing out one of the ways by which young people are lured to the dangerous disease that has eaten deeply into the society.[328] More recently Pope Benedict XVI speaking to representatives of world religions who at his invitation assembled at Assisi on October 27, 2011, the anniversary of the famous 1986 World Day of Prayer, pointed out that secularism or denial of God leads to many dangers including decline of humanity for unless man knows God and worships him, he cannot know and respect himself.[329]

Similar to the effects of the New Age and equally dangerous for the world is the proliferation of cults and sects—pseudo-religious movements. They not only draw Christians to their misleading movements, they also disturb the Church's dialogue with non-Christian religions. They do this first of all by giving non-Christian religions the impression that they are Christian groups. Then they proselytize in these religions without regard to human dignity. In addition, they cause friction with national or local governments by teaching their members categorically that they need not obey the law of the land, since they are subjects of God not of any human government. These movements are generally closed to logical reasoning and refuse to shift from their pre-conceived positions. While only some overtly practice occultism, all of them are closely related to atheism, for they are either themselves forms of atheism which sometimes put on a religious garb and deceive the uninformed, or they lead to atheism by causing confusion in the minds of their victims.[330]

The most prominent among these are, Jehovah's Witnesses, Christian Science, Mormonism (or Latter Day Saints), Spiritism (or Spiritualism which in all its many forms is occult or demonic), the Theosophical Society, Zen Buddhism, the Church of the New Jerusalem, the Bahai Faith, the Black Moslem Cult, and Anglo-Israelism.[331] We are not going to discuss each of these movements as such but will rather present briefly some of the problems they pose-not only to the Church and its membership but to society in general. Before we go on, let us see a brief description or definition of a cult or sect.

Cults, Sects and Their Characteristics

A cult or sect has been defined as "any religious group with a distinctive worldview of its own derived from, but not identical with the teaching of a major world religion."[332] In addition to this, a cult has a self-appointed messianic leader (or group of leaders), who focuses veneration on himself, claims divine selection, and wields autocratic control over members' lives. The methods used for the purpose of recruiting, retention and fund-raising are replete with deception and misrepresentation. And every cult uses techniques that are aimed at "controlling individual thought and personal privacy," which frequently leads to "a coerced reconstitution of personality."[333] A further explanation of this description may be helpful in understanding better the characteristics of a cult. First, the group has a charismatic leader (who may be the founder of the group or his successor) who seeks to draw all the attention of the group to himself rather than to God. Second, it uses a deceitful method of recruitment which gives the prospective recruit a false but attractive picture of the group, whose real name is often not disclosed early to the recruit. Third, the recruit is usually not given enough time to evaluate what is happening before he is initiated: the initiation process is very rapid. Fourth, the group tries to dissuade members who wish to leave it with threats of spiritual or physical harm. Fifth, there is lack of visible signs that the money collected is spent according to the intention of the donor; the leader (or leaders) usually lives in some sort of affluence while many members live in great poverty.[334]

Cults often have more recognizable peculiarities or traits: an inordinate obsession or preoccupation with fund-raising; the use of the mind manipulation or mind control method in recruitment and training, which tries to and often changes the person's personality; sudden and total separation from friends, family members or anyone who could change the adherent's mind; strong hatred for anyone who is not a member of the group; the demanding of complete obedience or submission from the recruit to even the least leader; the forfeiting of the right to leave the group.[335]

We shall use one or more of the groups mentioned above to illustrate some of these peculiarities. With regard to worldview or belief, the Jehovah's Witnesses, like other cults, deny the doctrine of the Trinity, the divinity of Christ, the physical resurrection and return of Christ in glory, eternal punishment, the reality of hell, the eternal existence or immortality of the soul, and many other major beliefs of the Christian religion. Their main preoccupation is with Armageddon or eschatological destruction which will bring an end to all the clergy in the Christian religion, all organized religions and other people who do not belong to the fold of the Jehovah's Witnesses.[336] By thus disposing of the major teachings of Christianity, especially eternal punishment, and by insisting on Armageddon, which will destroy the rest of the world apart from the Jehovah's Witnesses, they make their movement attractive to the uninformed, especially the young over whom they spread their dragnets. One of their ploys is the use of the apocalyptic writings of the Bible, especially the books of Daniel and Revelation, which neither they nor those they pretend to teach understand. They hold that 144,000 people will be saved. This number, according to them, is made up mainly of Jehovah's Witnesses.[337] The rest of mankind who are not destroyed by Armageddon will be allowed to reign in an earthly paradise for one thousand years.

Cults usually employ deceit and appeal to people's feelings and ignorance to gather members and make money. For instance, shortly after the First World War, just after people had seen the horrors and ruinous effects of war, the Witnesses launched a world-wide campaign with a slogan and booklet entitled, *Millions Now Living Will Never Die.* In this booklet the world was warned that it would be destroyed by 1925. But those who joined the Watch Tower organization or Jehovah's Witnesses would be spared. The booklet also held that Abraham, Isaac, Jacob, and other servants of God of the Old Testament would be resurrected that same year to usher in a righteous government headed by the Watch Tower Society.[338]

For the people of the world who had just suffered through a war that destroyed millions of human lives and whole cities, for people suffering from food shortage and other necessities of life, this message was electrifying. For the people badly needed a message of hope. Seizing upon the impetus generated by this message, the Watch Tower Society embarked upon worldwide sale or rather peddling of booklets and tracts published by the society. The aim was to raise millions of badly needed dollars. This task was to be accomplished by volunteers who came in great numbers. Before these set out in September 1922, they were carefully instructed to warn the world of the end of time in 1925. Many Watch Tower members and recruits, now convinced that the world was about to be destroyed, sold their homes and businesses and became volunteers who peddled the booklets from door to door, not only throughout the United States but also to different parts of other lands. So total was the conviction of members of the Watch Tower society about the false prophecy regarding 1925 that many farmers did not plant their crops that spring. And when 1925 came and went and this prediction was not fulfilled, as would be expected, many people were disappointed. The leader of the Watch Tower Society, Joseph Franklin Rutherford, who had succeeded the founder, Charles Taze Russell, blamed the discouragement that followed this disappointment on the devil.[339] The crash of the stock market of 1929 and the depression that followed in its aftermath offered the Witnesses another opportunity to preach on the end time. They pointed out that the depression was a sign of the nearness of the end of time. Since many people were unhappy and unemployed, many joined the Watch Tower Society. The main work of these newcomers was to peddle the society's booklets from door to door. A lot of money was made and many new members recruited.[340]

Leader's Affluent Living

As indicated above, while most cult members live in relative poverty, their leader usually has an affluent life-style. This was exemplified in the lifestyle of Joseph Rutherford, the second president of the Watch Tower Society. While many members forfeited good meals and decent shelters making millions of dollars for the society by peddling the tracts or booklets of the society, their leader lived like a wealthy king. In 1929 he bought a large piece of land in an exclusive residential part of San Diego. California. Here he commissioned a palatial home to be built. In those depression years when a very nice home could be purchased for 3,000 to 5,000 dollars, the construction of Rutherford's palace cost 75,000 dollars. The home was completed in 1930 and Rutherford spent his winters there until his death in 1942. He called the home *Beth Sarim* or the *House of Princes,* thus named because he convinced his followers that the end was close and that the home was built for the ancient princes, such as Abraham, Jacob, and David, who would occupy the house when they resurrected. In order further to authenticate his conviction about this matter he dratted an unusual property deed or agreement. According to this, the property was deeded to the Watch Tower and Tract Society to be held in trust for these ancient princes. The home would be turned over to them as soon as they appeared and identified themselves. But before they would come Rutherford would make the exclusive use of the property. Having finished the palace, Rutherford bought two very expensive and luxurious 16-cylinder Cadillac vehicles, each of which cost at least nine times as much as an ordinary car at the time. One of these was at San Diego and the other at the Brooklyn headquarters. These vehicles, according to Rutherford, were provided to facilitate transportation for the princes of old. However, before their appearance, only the president would make use of these vehicles.[341]

Rutherford spent the winters at Beth Sarim and traveled by steamship to Europe every summer. At Brooklyn he maintained a luxurious apartment, drank alcohol prodigiously, enjoyed quality cigars and the company of traveling female companions, all during the depression when many people in America depended on soup kitchens for their daily sustenance.[342] Rutherford's lifestyle, as indicated above, is only an example of the usual lifestyle of leaders of cults and sects.

Why Fraud or Deception Succeeds in Cults and Sects

From September 30 to October 3, 1984, fifty members and former members of the Jehovah's Witnesses staged a protest or open demonstration against this pseudo-religious body. Some of their placards read: "This Religion is a Snare and a Danger." "I Gave Up Babies," "1884 to 1984: A Century of False Prophecies and Oppression" "Free After 43 Years," "50 Years: Why Did I Leave?"[343] Most of these demonstrators had suffered unnecessarily because of their strict adherence to the teaching of this society. Some were told not to marry because the end was very close; and some who were already married were told not have children but to spend the remaining time working for Jehovah and his Witnesses. Some were imprisoned while following the society's teaching which indoctrinated them to disobey the law of the land. Others had been disfellowshipped or excommunicated because they had associated with people who were not members of the society, while others still had lost their babies because the teaching of the Witnesses forbade blood transfusion even to the babies who badly needed it.[344]

A question that seems in order here is, why did these members still remain with the Witnesses after so many years of deceit, false prophecies, and hypocrisy? Or rather, why do people continue their membership in cults and sects even when the teachings or activities of these movements no longer seem credible or acceptable to a normal thinking person? In the answer to this question lies much of the secret of the continuance and growth of these new religious movements.

The first answer to this question is that all cultic belief systems employ institutional dogmatism to control the minds of their members. For instance, the Watch Tower Society or Jehovah Witnesses, brainwashes it members to believe that God himself rules over the movement through its president and officers of the Watch Tower in Brooklyn, New York, and that the movement is the visible representative of God on earth. For members are made to believe that Jesus began his reign as king invisibly in the world in 1914; that he needed an organization to announce his kingdom and administer his interests. In 1919, they hold, Jesus carefully examined all the Christian denominations but rejected them, choosing rather the Watch Tower Society or Jehovah's Witnesses. The Governing Body, the body that rules the Watch Tower Society, and the brain behind all its manipulations and brainwashing, claims to receive the jurisdiction over Jesus' organization in order to maintain purity of doctrine. With this as its starting point, this body can teach anything to its members and nobody is expected to object or protest, since the teaching is supposed to come from Jesus or God himself.[345] Brainwashing of members is not peculiar to Jehovah's Witnesses; other cults do the same. And they all demand that their members remain loyal even to the point of surrendering themselves completely to the cause of the cult, thereby leaving their life or death at the disposal of the leaders. This blind surrender has resulted in many mass disasters. For often some leaders, for reasons best known to themselves, have caused the deaths of many of the members. An example is the death of more than nine hundred members and some leaders of a cult in Uganda in March 2000. More than three hundred died in the fire purposely set by the group itself on a building inside which the members were gathered; the rest had been murdered earlier before the arson. According to information from several sources, the cult leader had convinced his followers that the world would end in 1999. Most of the members therefore surrendered their belongings to him. When, by the year 2000, his prediction was found to be false, some of the members lost faith in him and demanded the return of their belongings. The leader himself got frustrated and murdered many through various means and finished the rest by gathering them inside their meeting hall and setting the house on fire. He was believed to have invoked the authority of Jesus to commit these crimes.[346]

And it is good to know that the Jesus of the cults is not the Jesus of Christians. Their Jesus is what St. Paul calls "another Jesus" (2 Cor, 11:4), and they are the false apostles, deceitful workers who mask, themselves as apostles of Christ (2 Cor. 11:13). The Christian Jesus is the one we have already described earlier in this book. He is true God and true man, of the same substance and equal with the Father. Cults generally do not admit that Jesus is God. Some of them call him an angel or spirit. For instance, Jehovah's Witnesses, like the heretic Arius of the fourth century, misinterpret Colossians 1:15; they see Christ as the first of all creatures, son of God but not God and not equal with the Father.[347] They reference this to Revelation 3:14, which calls Christ the source (in Jehovah's Witnesses Bible translated as the beginning) of God's creation. They fail to understand that by applying the phrase 'first of all creation' to Christ Paul means to indicate Christ's pre-existence and preeminence over all creatures, which is indicated in verse 18 of the same chapter. And verse 19 goes further to show that Jesus is true God by stating, "in him all the fullness of God was pleased to dwell."

As a corollary to the first answer above, it must be noted that the cultic belief system is close-minded; cult members are not interested in rational evaluation of facts. The cultic structure interprets the facts for the members, usually by invoking the Bible or the respective founders as the ultimate source of their interpretation or pronouncement. The Watch Tower Society, for instance, sees also the source of the authority of its Governing Body from the Bible. It claims that this body received this authority from Jesus and that it is the "faithful and prudent servant" that is referred to in Matthew 24:25—"Who, then, is the faithful and prudent servant whom the master has put in charge of his Household . . ."[348] The result of this close-mindedness is that cultists, such as the Witnesses, hardly shift to logical reasoning or logical consistency; they do not listen to sound argument or to any advice unless it is given by a cult member, especially the leaders. Not only this, they are drilled to hate anybody who holds opposing beliefs; they are formed to hate especially both the true Christian message and Christians and to believe that they have been freed from Christian bondage and exploitation.[349]

Cults usually employ not only oral teaching but also their writings to drill or condition their members to respond or react negatively to the outside world, to those who do not belong to their group. For instance, Jehovah's Witnesses use the literature of the Watch Tower to condition their members to see the Church and Christians as agents of the devil, hypocrites and haters of God. Thus they condition these members to hate Christians who they believe hate God or Jehovah and his people, the Witnesses. They condemn to God's anger and vengeance Christians and all who do not belong to their cult.[350]

Reasons for the Spread of Secularism, Cults and Sects

The factors that help the spread or increase of these threats can be divided into two broad groups. The first group consists of the techniques or efforts the new religious movements make for their own growth. Making up the second group are external factors that help them and secularism to spread. Each of these groups has within itself so many more factors or sub-factors that to discuss all of them even in brief detail will require writing a separate book on the subject. Let us, however, now see very briefly a few of the main factors in each of these groups.

a) The Techniques of the New Religious Movements.

We have noted earlier that cults and sects do not tell most of their members the truth: many of those who belong to these cults do not know the history and real background of the movement they belong to. They are convinced that they belong to a Christian church. And usually cults and sects make their movements attractive by teaching only what they think people would like to hear. For instance, many of them reject the existence of hell, and insist that only those who join their cult will have the fullness of happiness. One common feature of all of them, including even those which pretend to be Christian, is their failure to identify who Jesus really is. For their understanding of Jesus is quite different from the Christian understanding, even though one often hears them call on Jesus. There are many other things they do to promote their groups. Here we shall discuss very briefly only three of them. These three are: i) training and commitment to proselytism. ii) use of cult/sect literature, and iii) support. i) *Training and commitment to Proselytism:* Fast-growing cults and sects take time to train their members to be committed to spreading their mission or the mission of their prophets. The Mormons, for example, start very early to train their children. In most places where there are many of them they have their own schools where only their children can be taught or brought up in the Mormon way of life. They convince their members that theirs is the only true religion which has a mission to convert most people in the world to this new religious movement. They train their recruits and their young people to be committed to the mission of the movement. To deepen this commitment, after their training, especially young adult members (young men and women ages 20 to 23), usually spend two years of their lives doing cult missionary work in a foreign country or at least in another place far from their home, and they do this at their own expense. Each is prepared to be a good salesman for the cult by being good-mannered, gentle and hospitable. And what they are to sell is the mission of their cult. They are trained very well in their dogmas and how to use the Bible to convince or confuse the ignorant, many of them Christians.[351]

Zeal for cult missionary activity is not exclusive to Mormons: most other cults and sects do the same. Who has not encountered the over-zealousness of Jehovah's Witnesses? The amazing impudence with which they confront even strangers, intrude upon people's time without invitation or warning, and the enthusiasm with which they distribute their literature, are signs of their zeal for the growth of their cult. One of the distinguishing characteristics of the members of the Jehovah's Witnesses cult is their ability to handle the Scriptures. Any of them can use the Scripture to embarrass or confuse an average Christian, even though most of their quotations or citations are usually out of context. Usually, before they set out for their proselytizing mission, they meet together to prepare their themes as well as the Scripture passages that may have connection with these themes. Then they boldly go from door to door seeking recruits. When they encounter Christians and other non-members they present their subject or subjects and support them with the already prepared Scripture passages to the amazement of many an ignorant Christian. Usually carrying a text called *Emphatic Diglot* which has interlinear readings of the Greek they pretend to know the original language of the New Testament. They and other cultists know that many Christians are poorly informed or catechized in the truths they are supposed to believe in. Hence they swoop on these Christians, promising to help them see the light. They invite the Christians for a short discussion on the Bible. Or they may express the wish to visit again for the same purpose. Once this chance is given, they start at once to sow their seeds of confusion and blindness. Often they will not accept the first *no* for an answer. They usually persist and this sometimes ends in their favor. The zeal of Jehovah's Witnesses and Mormons for spreading their message is shared by other cults and sects which accounts much for their fast growth. One advice that Christians who encounter Jehovah's Witnesses and other cultists should hold fast to is insisting on the divinity of Christ and his equality with the Father. Let them not discuss the Bible with these cults, because that will hardly yield any positive result. ii) *Use of Cult/Sect Literature:* The second tool of the cults for the propagation of their message is the dissemination of their literature. In many countries religious literature which many ordinary people are longing for is very scarce. Cults are aware of this. They therefore inundate many countries with cult magazines and tracts. Probably it is difficult to find any village anywhere in the world (except in Moslem and Hindu territories) where the copies of the Jehovah's Witnesses' *Watch Tower* and *Awake* magazines are not yet distributed. Every year several million copies of these magazines are printed. These are either peddled from door to door as we have said before or they are mailed from Brooklyn, New York to every continent. In their desire to get converts, they sometimes distribute these magazines and other pieces of cult literature free. They go as far as translating their literature to the vernacular, the language of the people, especially in places where English is not the common language. This works; they ensnare many people, especially the young.[352] iii) *Support.* Many cults and sects have various ways of helping their members or prospective members. I have chosen to put these various ways of helping under the generic term, *support.* These various ways are very many and we have only to mention just a few here. We know that the world in which we live today is full of pains and hurts; many people need support, moral, social economic, and otherwise. Cults often seem to provide the help badly needed not only to their members but also to prospective members thereby luring them into their movement. In many places cults and sects take time to seek out those in any kind of need, for instance, a lonely widow or a family in distress. They endeavor to offer help. But this help is not a disinterested humanitarian or charitable act. It is aimed at converting the beneficiary to their cult or sect. Once they have won the confidence of the beneficiary, the next step is to present the message of their movement.

Even though in many cults and sects the leaders live in some kind of affluence at the expense of the members, some of the movements, however, have well-planned social welfare programs that not only induce their members to remain faithful to the movement but also attracts outsiders to their group. This is especially true of the Mormon cult. If a Mormon family has reverses of fortune or financial hardship, for instance, in the event of loss of the job or injury or death of the "bread winner," the cult undertakes to care and provide for the family. In any kind of crisis, when many other people may be in dire need of the basic necessities, Mormons fare well because of their social welfare program.[353]

Included in the help or support that the cults claim to offer are their counseling or healing programs. This holds true especially of the spiritist or spiritualist cults, cults whose members are generally mediums, witches and others who deal with the spirits of the dead and other discarnate spirits. In their séances spiritists claim to "incorporate" or unite to themselves some discarnate spirits which become their guides during these séances. Probably the most typical of these spiritist cults are those of Brazil. Spiritist cultists in Brazil number more than three million. There, four major spiritist cults exist, which sprang from the Yoruba tradition of West Africa. These four are *Candomble, Umbanda, Quimbanda,* and *Kardecism.* As is usual with cults, their religious sessions are full of syncretistic practices. Candomble, the oldest of them, uses Yoruba names for the spirits. Fortunes are told by cowry shells, and women called the "Mothers of the Saints" conduct the religious services including telling fortunes for their clients, many of whom are Christians.[354]

Unlike Candomble, Umbanda uses more of Christian names than of Yoruba names. Each practitioner or member, depending on his/her birth date, is assigned to one of the seven *lines* or sub-groups into which the cult is organized. The one thus assigned a sub-group adopts the paraphernalia (foods, colors, numbers, charts, perfumes, incense, symbols) of that sub-group. Here both men and women can preside or lead in the services. The services which include "healing" are held in locations called "Casas Umbando," and involve the "incorporation" by "priests" and "priestesses" of minor spirits such as the "Old Black Ones" (spirits of deceased black slaves) or the "Indians of the Seven Arrows" (spirits of the deceased original inhabitants of the land). After the "incorporation" the presiders are considered ready to "heal." In these sessions there are a lot of dancing and other entertainment which sometimes seem to provide some emotional or psychological healing for some clients.[355]

These cultists claim they can place a curse on a person and can also remove a curse placed by themselves or by others. Lamentably many of their clients are Christians who go to them in droves and often join them. Francis MacNutt narrates the story of a case he met in Bogota, Columbia. Here a Christian woman living in a so-called Christian community took her son who had a serious and mysterious illness to a spiritist. After she had paid the fee the spiritist told her that her next-door neighbor who was angry with this woman had asked him to put a curse on the boy. It was then that the boy became sick. After the curse the boy became well again. And ironically, the woman, her next-door neighbor and the spiritist were all nominal Christians.[356] One can see that they were Christians by name but were all involved in cultist practices. Christians join such cults by consulting the cultists in their times of great need.

b) External Factors Which Promote Secularism, Cults and Sects

One of the greatest factors here is the expulsion of God from public schools. How can we give sound education to our children when we fail to teach them about God and religious principles on which good moral life is usually founded? Most of those who claim they have no religion or who join cults are people who did not receive good religious education during their school years. Some of them were former Catholics who have lost their true faith. Ironically, a good number of them accept the palatable or painless dogmas of some cults and join them, while others remain without any form of worship or religious affiliation. The question here is, apart from the absence of religious education in public schools, why do we lose many Christians to secularism and pseudo-religious movements? Why do many former Catholics who join cults and sects seem to find in these movements the satisfaction which they seemed not to have found in the Church? To put this in other words, why are so many Catholics only nominal Christians and lack conviction? Let us consider just a few reasons.

i) *Omissions of the Family and of the Church.*

A number of factors have contributed to the growth of secularism and to nominal Catholicism today. These factors too are many but we shall see only a few of them here.

One of these is the failure of many families in their duty. It has been observed that a good number of Catholic couples now care little about the spiritual welfare of their children. Many of those who have their children baptized care little about bringing them up as good Catholics. Some of them send their children to religious education classes at the church but do not care to take these children to Mass on Sunday nor do they make any effort to evangelize or catechize the children at home. Children are now taught by the television instead of by their parents. That is why most of them can recite the television commercials before they start grade school while few know even the basic prayers. In addition, many parents pretend to be respecting the freedom of their children to choose their religion when they come of age, and hence they fail to educate the children in the faith. To make things worse, divorce and remarriage, especially in the West, are now seen as normal and thus many children have been uprooted, left hanging, as it were, and confused. For, little or no religious education is given to children from such broken homes. [357]

Not only families have failed. A lot of parishes have their share of the blame. Catholics in many places are denied the opportunity to know Jesus and worship him in the Eucharist through the Holy Hour, Benediction, Eucharistic procession, Forty Hours Adoration and similar devotions. And the use of the sacramentals, such as holy water, medals, scapulars, the rosary; and other traditional devotions that supported the faith have been done away with in many Catholic homes and churches in the West. Since the disappearance of many of these traditional devotions the spiritual hunger which they helped to alleviate is intensified; many Christians now see their religion or worship very dry and unattractive. Some of these join cults and sects. Add to this the fact that children are not instructed that it is wrong to miss Mass on Sunday without adequate or good reason.

Another serious way that some churches or parishes have promoted the growth of secularism and cults is in the area of formation and ongoing education of Christians. A lot of harm has already been done to a good number of Christians by poor or bad formation. A careful observation today will notice that in a number of parishes there are good and God-fearing religious educators who know their job and enjoy doing it. But in other parishes those entrusted with religious education are not the right people. Some of them have lost their own faith; a few have good will but are ignorant, while the rest are those who have one grievance or another against the Church.[358] How can such men and women raise up our children in the faith? Many a pastor often has no time to see how things are going in his parish's school of religion. Many of the children are badly taught or fed with wrong material.

Very disturbing is the fact that some of those who fall into the dreadful anomalies we mentioned above are people newly initialed into the Church, who have seen very little of the Church. Neophytes who defect are usually those not properly prepared according to the Church's directive before their initiation. The Church has instructed that adults or children who are admitted into the Church today be well formed by using properly the Rite of Christian Initiation of Adults (R.C.I.A.). How many parishes are using this rite today as the Church wants it to be used? It is sad that in many parishes this rite is not used at all: in others, it is very poorly used. In these parishes little instruction is given and hardly are the rituals part of the formation except in the rites of passage, namely, the rite of acceptance into the order of the catechumens, the rite of election and the sacraments of initiation. This poor, haphazard formation is not what was envisaged by the Church when that rite was rediscovered and restored. And such alone cannot form responsible and strong Christians. In addition, after initiation in most cases nothing more is done to help the growth of the faith of the neophytes; the critical ongoing education of Christians both old and young is abandoned. And it has been determined that a good number of the Catholics who fall into secularism or join cults and sects were those who grew up with the little or no religious education they received as children. As they grow up mentally and physically, they discover that their religious education is not adequate to their adult life; a religious vacuum is created in such people. Since their church or parish does not provide ongoing adult education, they make one of two choices. Either they opt to live without any religion at all or they choose to join fundamentalists, cults and sects. When, therefore, we poorly form adults and children in the faith we are simply promoting secularism, cults and sects.

An important part of the ongoing formation of Christians is the homily of the Sunday Mass. But often too, the homily is poorly prepared and boring, leaving most of the people empty or dry and causing some of them to form the opinion that the homily is not an important part of the Mass. Such people complain even when a constructive homily lasts up to ten minutes or when such homilies challenge them to live the Christian life they committed themselves to at baptism. They always want only homilies tailored according to their tastes or whims. Such Christians continue to grow drier and drier until they no longer see why they should continue to belong to the Church. And they are easily too, lost to secularism, cults and sects.

The poor formation of many Catholics is one of the most serious reasons for their lack of commitment to the Church's cause. Very few in many parishes are ready to be involved in the Church's spiritual and corporal works of mercy; few are interested in the lay apostolate as the Church demands. Much of this is left to the priest alone so that often he has little or no time for other pastoral activities. Even in the liturgy, many are not willing to play their own role in the Mass. A good number of those who want to help in the liturgy are interested only in the priest's role. Is it not a common phenomenon in some parishes to see more people interested in the Eucharistic ministry than being in the choir or in the proclaiming of the word as lectors? And among those interested in the Eucharistic ministry only few are willing to take Communion to the sick or homebound. Because of this failure of many Christians to play their roles in the liturgy, Sunday Masses often look like funeral rites with little singing and other signs of joy. This has disgusted many young Christians who enjoy active and joyful liturgy. Many have left the Church also to join cults, sects and fundamentalists who provide them with lively singing and even dancing in their worship.[359]

Owing probably to this failure of the Christian faithful to play their role and make things lighter for the pastor, or perhaps due to the fact that some priests were not trained to give pastoral care to the parishioners apart from the sacraments, many priests do not make time to listen to their parishioners. An experienced pastor knows that the priest's pastoral care can save a lot of trouble for individuals and families. Many, though not all, cases taken to psychologists or psychiatrists can better be treated by an experienced pastor. Some of these may be spiritual rather than psychological or psychiatric problems where the priest should be the expert. But often psychology alone is enthroned at the expense of biblical and theological knowledge and pastoral care. Unfortunately this has led some priests to believe that their pastoral care or prayer for some parishioners cannot bear visible fruit.[360] As a consequence of this neglect, some Christians seek spiritual help from wrong hands, such as cults and occultists, who often convert them to their pseudo-religion. Christians should solve spiritual problems through their own religion, not through cults or devil worshippers. Thomas Sullivan, Jr., the fourteen-year-old eight grader, whom we mentioned in the early part of this chapter, would have been helped if a competent priest was available and consulted.

Unfortunately, many pastors deny the existence and activities of the devil or evil spirits; even when their parishioners are under demonic attack or oppression. To such priests talking about the devil seems naive and a return to medieval thinking. A parish where parishioners do not know where to go when under demonic attack is cheated and unfortunate. Remember that we are not advocating seeing the devil everywhere. This would be wrong and contrary to the teaching of the Church. And it would be equally wrong to deny the existence or activity of the devil in the world. The Bible teaches that the devil is always active in the world. It calls him by various names, such as Satan, the Adversary, "the god of this world", "the prince of this world", and other names. It warns us not to be ignorant of his activities. The Christian, however, is provided with weapons which can be useful in fighting this deadly enemy and his followers.[361]

Moreover the Magisterium or teaching authority of the Catholic Church has always taught that the devil exists and does a lot of harm to individuals and groups. About the year 1886, for instance, Pope Leo XIII sent to all dioceses of the Catholic Church general prayers of exorcism which before the changes of the Second Vatican Council were said by the priest and congregation after every Mass. It was a plea to God through the intercession of Mary and St. Michael, the prince of the heavenly host, to send Satan and his hosts back to hell.[362] And in his general audience of November 15, 1972, Pope Paul VI stressed that the devil is a real enemy that causes harm to individuals and society. He insists that one of the greatest challenges of the Church and Christians is to find defense against the devil. He insists that "evil is not merely a lack of something, but an effective agent, a living spiritual being, perverted and perverting." The pope makes it clear that it is contrary to the teaching of the Church and Bible to refuse to recognize the devil or to explain it away "as a pseudo-reality, a conceptual and fanciful personification of the unknown causes of our misfortunes."[363] Three years after this statement, the Sacred Congregation for the Divine Worship issued a document, "Christian Faith and Demonology", giving in greater detail and reaffirming the traditional teaching of the Church on the devil and the harm he can cause in the world.[364] These are only a few examples. Pastors and others entrusted with the care of souls should be aware of this danger and find ways of protecting those under their care.

ii) *Scandal.*

Scandal in the Church has contributed much to the growth of secularism and cults. Especially since the past forty years, many priests and religious have abandoned their vocation. A good number of others have been accused of one immoral act or another, and sometimes these accusations or allegations are blown out of proportion by the social media.

Worse still many so-called Catholic theologians or rather scholars now impudently and openly oppose the Magisterium or teaching authority of the Church. They arrogate to themselves the teaching role of the pope, and inform Christians that they do not need to accept the teaching of the pope. They wrongly invoke the Second Vatican Council as opening the door to democracy in the Church.[365] But they fail to read the council's statement about the absolute authority of the pope even over the college of bishops of the universal Church: "The college of bishops has for all that no authority unless united with the Roman Pontiff, Peter's successor, as its head, whose primatial authority, let it be added, over all, whether pastors or faithful remains in its integrity."[366] If the council declares even the authority of the college of bishops, unless united with the pope as its head, null and void, how can these theologians claim that the same council opened the door to them to oppose the pope, claim his teaching authority and inform Christians to reject his teaching? Every sincere Christian should not allow himself to be deluded by the false teachings of these theologians. The pope and the bishops in full communion with him are the successors of Peter and other Apostles to whom Christ gave the authority to shepherd his flock, the Church, as we noted earlier in this book. Where do the erring theologians get their own authority? They simply want to cause confusion or dissension in the Church. They have already succeeded in this to some extent; for, owing to the confusion and discontent they incited among many Catholics, some have fallen back into secularism or joined cults and sects. But let all be reminded here that any Christian who follows the teaching of these erring theologians purposely wants to go wrong, for they have no teaching authority.

As dreadful as the confusion caused by erring theologians is the seed of disloyalty that feminism is sowing in the Church. Feminism, in its ordinary form, is in the family of the New Age movement or pagan worship. Its main aim is not the liberation of women as it often claims; its adherents are first of all devoted to the "goddess" who is found in themselves and in nature. This movement often has little to do with issues of fair play, issues that the Catholic Church usually champions. Its main desire is to dethrone God from heaven and install "the mother goddess". Members support abortion on demand and lesbian rights.[367] They now have many members in the Church.

Their main mode of operation in the Church is to create discontent, promote resentment, frustration, and a false sense of persecution by the Church which they see as male-dominated.[368] They usually hate any man in authority in the Church, unless he leans toward their belief and aspirations. Many of their members are Catholic nuns. These attend feminist conventions where they and other witches or priestesses plan their mode of attack on the Church or of causing trouble and confusion in it. A good number of these so-called nuns and other women in their movement are given important functions in the Church. Some are administrators or classroom teachers, while others are in charge of parish religious education. Through their functions they foster the agenda of their movement in the Church. Sometimes they either enlist into their movement some of the children entrusted to their care or so cause discontent, disloyalty and confusion in the minds of the men and women they work with that these defect to secularism or cultism.[369] Many pastors are either unaware of this intrigue or they are so intimidated by the feminists working with them that they remain silent. In whichever case, secularism and pseudo-religious movements gain at the expense of the Church.

What Can Be Done to Save the Situation?

We have seen the enormity of the threat secularism, cults and sects pose for the Church and the world, and the factors that promote their growth. The ways to check these forces are many. Some suggestions have already been indirectly given above when we were treating some of the factors that promote the forces or movements under discussion. Here I shall briefly make a few more suggestions.

The first of these is formation of Christians. Those to be initiated into the Church must be properly formed before they receive the sacraments of initiation. The Church has already provided the program for the formation. What is required is for parishes to begin to use it in the right way. This program, if properly used, prepares adults and children in such a way that they usually become such strong Christians that it is difficult for cults and similar forces to shake their faith. In addition, they are prepared to be zealous evangelizers, so that the evangelized becomes the evangelizer. Their new zeal also affects or warms up older Christians who may be growing cold in their own faith. In this way the whole parish can be revived.[370] But the formation should not stop after initiation. The ongoing education of both the old and the young in the parish helps much to strengthen the faith. Part of this formation should also include cautious enlightenment about cults. This is to prepare Christians against the inroads of these deadly enemies.

Important also for the Church at this time is the implementation of the new evangelization which Pope John Paul II frequently reiterated. This is a plan of the Church to re-evangelize Christians throughout the world or deepen their faith so that they in turn can join in the work of evangelizing the rest of the world. It forms the core of the pope's plan for the convocation of a special assembly or synod of bishops for each of the continents of the world. In these synods directives are given as to the way to renew the Church in the third millennium and every Christian is invited to be part of the renewal process.[371] If the recommendations made in these synods are followed, and the few observations made in this chapter are given serious consideration, the Church will be much renewed, and Christians, instead of falling prey to secularism and cults, will be better prepared to convert not only adherents of non-Christian religions but also cultists and those who have no religion or deny the existence of God.

NOTES

1   Vatican II, *Nostra Aetate (Declaration on the Relation of the Church to Non-Christian Religions)* #1.

2   Ibid..

3   Pietro Rossano, "Christ's Lordship and Religious Pluralism in Roman Catholic Perspective" in *Christ's Lordship and Religions Pluralism,* ed. Gerald H. Anderson and Thomas F. Stransky (Maryknoll, New York: Orbis Books, 1981), p. 97.

4   Ibid. pp. 97-98.

5   Vatican 11. *Nostra Aetate #2.*

6   Vatican II, *Ad Gentes (Decree on the Church's Missionary Activity)* #11.

7   Vatican II, *Nostra Aetate* #2. See also idem, *Lumen Gentium (Constitution on the Church)* #17.

8   Pope John Paul II, *Redemptor Hominis* (Washington D.C. :Office of Publishing Services, United States Catholic Conference, 1979), #11.

9   Pope John Paul II, Ibid. #1

10   Pietro Rossano, locus cit. pp. 99.

11   Cardinal Francis Arinze, "Interreligious Dialogue: Problems, Prospects, and Possibilities" [here-in-after: "Interreligious

Dialogue"] (Paper read at the celebration of the 150th anniversary of Nashville Diocese, Nashville, Tennessee, 19 March 1987), P. 3.

12   Ibid. pp. 4-6.

13   Ibid. p. 3.

14   Pontifical Council for Interreligious Dialogue and the Congregation for the Evangelization of Peoples, "Dialogue and Proclamation", *Origins 16* [weekly journal] (Catholic News Service, United States Catholic Conference, Washington D.C., July 4): 124.

15   Ibid. pp. 3-4.

16   Walbert Buhlmann, *The Coming of the Third Church* (Maryknoll, New York: Orbis Books, 1977), p.27.

17   See Wilfred Cantwell Smith, *The Faith of Other men* (New York: New American Library, 1963), p.11.

18   In 1970 Christians constituted 33.9% of the world population; Catholics alone made up 18. 5%. See David Barrett, ed. *Christian Encyclopedia* (Nairobi: Oxford University Press, 1982), p. 6; see also Buhlmann, op. cit. p. 143.

19   Arinze, "Interreligious Dialogue", p.7.

20   Ibid. p.10.

21   Pope John Paul II, "The Challenge and Possibility of Peace" [The Pope's address at Assisi on the World Day of Prayer October 27, 1986] *Origins* 16 (November 6, 1986): 370-371.

22   Ibid.

23   Arinze, "Interreligious Dialogue" pp. 8-9; quotation on p. 9. See also Vatican II, *Lumen Gentium,* #13.

24   Pope John XXIII, "The Council—at the Threshold of a New Era" [the opening address of the Second Vatican Council], *The Pope Speaks* 8(1963):213.

25   Pope Paul VI, *Ecclesiam Suam,* (Boston: Daughters of St. Paul, 1964), p. 72.

26   Vatican II, *Gaudium et Spes (Constitution on the Church in the Modern World)* #92; see also Pope Paul VI, *Ecclesiam Suam* #76.

27   Pope John Paul II, "The Meaning of the Assisi Day of Prayer" [address to the Roman Curia on December 22, 1986] *Origins* 16 (January 15, 1987):561.

28   It is true that Pope VI in 1 964 visited Jerusalem and spoke in a friendly manner to the Jews there cf. *The Pope Speaks* 9(winter 1 964):226-227, but the real positive relations of the Church with the Jews started with *Nostra Aetate.*

29   Vatican II, Nostra Aetate, #4.

30   Ibid.

31   Ibid.

32   Following this example, similar liaison groups or committees have been formed nationally and internationally, between the Jews and international church bodies, such as the World Council of Churches, the Church of England, the Lutheran World Federation, and the Orthodox churches. See Cardinal Johannes Willebrands, "Christians and Jews: A New Vision", in *Vatican II Revisited* ed. Alberic Stacpoole (Minneapolis: Winston Press, 1986), p. 227.

[33] Ibid. p. 227.

[34] The document is dated December, 1974, but published on January 3, 1975. The text is found in *Vatican Council II,* new rev. ed. Austin Flannery (Collegeville, Mn: Liturgical Press, 1984), pp. 743-749. [Here-in-after the document will often be designated simply as the "Guidelines"].

[35] Ibid. pp. 744-745.

[36] Ibid. pp. 745-746.

[37] Ibid. pp. 746-747

[38] Ibid. p. 748

[39] The text with the caption "The Jews and Judaism in Preaching and Catechesis" is found in *Origins* 15(July 4, 1985): 102-107. [Here-in-after often designated simply as the *Notes.*]

[40] Ibid. p. 103.

[41] Ibid. p.103.

[42] Ibid. p. 107. Marcion was a second-century heretic who rejected the Old Testament and part of the New Testament as the work of a demiurge, an evil god.

[43] 16 Ibid. p. 104-105.

[44] Ibid. p. 105.

[45] Ibid. p. 106.

46   Ibid. p. 107. It must be pointed out here that The International Jewish Committee on inter—religious Consultations expressed dissatisfaction with the contents of the *Notes*. It was of the view that some of its statements represent a regression from the earlier Catholic statements, such as *Nostra Aetate* and the *Guidelines..* The committee was dissatisfied with, among other things, the formulations about the Jews, Judaism, and Israel, which it said were described or defined in terms of Christian categories instead of the Jewish understanding of them, ibid p. 102. In July 23, 1985 a group of Jewish and Christian leaders also not quite satisfied with some sections of the same document, met in New York and jointly issued a statement to the effect that "The Notes" must be read in the context of the earlier Catholic documents, such as "Nostra Aetate" and "The Guidelines". See *Origins* 15(September 26. 1985):240.

47   The way Catholics now understand Jews and Judaism is reflected in the revised general intercessions of Good Friday liturgy, which now prays for the "Jewish people, the first to hear the word of God, that they may continue to grow in the love of his name and in faithfulness to his covenant." See *The Sacramentary: The Roman Missal, Revised by the Decree of the Second Vatican Council and Published by Authority of Pope Paul VI* (New York: Catholic Book Publishing Co., 1985), p. 153; also *Wikipedia, the Free Encyclopedia* sv. "Relations between Catholicism and Judaism."

48   *The Pope Speaks* 9 (winter 1964):267

49   Cardinal Johannes Willebrands [former president of the Vatican Commission for Religious Relations with the Jews], "A Matter of the Church's Identity", *Origins* 15(December 15. 1985):413-414

50   Pope John Paul II. "Dialogue: The Road to Understanding," *Origins* 10(December 4, 1980):399-400.

51   Ibid. p.400.

52   Ibid. p. 399.

53   Pope John Paul 11, "The importance of Jewish-Christian Relations", *Origins* 11 (March 25. 1982):660.

54   Ibid.

55   "The Pope Visits Rome's Chief Synagogue", *Origins* 15(April 24, 1986):731-732.

56   "Jews and Christians Share much together" Pope John II's general audience on April 28, 1999, *L'Osservatare Romano* 18(May5, 1999), p. 11.

57   *Catholic New York* September 13, 1990, p. 7.

58   Cardinal Joannes Willebrands, "Christians and Jews: A New Vision" in *Vatican II Revisited,* ed. Alberic Stacpoole (Minneapolis: Winston Press, 1986): 229.

59   *The Catholic World Report* 9(July 1999):1

60   *Catholic Sentinel,* [Portland, Oregon] 15 October 1999, p. 2. See also *The Tablet* [Brooklyn, New York]1 December 1990, p. 8.

61   "Christians close churches to protest mosque deal". *The Bulletin* [Bend, Oregon] Tuesday 23 November 1999, p. A5.

62   See *Wikipedia, the Free Encyclopedia* s.v. "Relations between Catholicism and Judaism."

63   "The Pope Visits Rome's Chief Synagogue", *Origins* 15(April 24, 1986): 731-732.

64   Pope John Paul II speaking in Rome in 1982 to experts in Jewish-Christian relations makes it clear that "clarity and awareness of our Christian identity are an essential basis for achieving authentic, fruitful and lasting relationships with the Jewish people"; see Pope John Paul, "The Importance of Jewish-Christian Relations", *Origins* 11{March25, 1982):660.

65   *Origins* 23(Jan. 13, 1994):525-528.

66   Origins 24(June 23,1994):82. Some may wonder why this diplomatic relation is important in the Jewish—Christian dialogue. It must be recalled that the government of the State of Israel belongs to the Jews, and the Vatican is the capital seat of the government of the universal Church.

67   *National Catholic Register* vol. 76 No. 14 April 2-8, 2000, pp. 1 & 7.

68   Apart from the Jews there are also, Moslems, Buddhists, Hindus—and each of these has multiple families. There are also, traditional religions, notably in Africa, Chinese folk religions, Shamanists, Confucians, Sikhs, Shinto's, Baha'is, Jains, and many others. See David Barret, op. cit. p.6.

69   Cardinal Francis Arinze, "The Urgency of Dialogue with Non-Christians", *Origins* 14(March 14, 1985):643,646.

70   Ibid. pp. 644-645.

71   Ibid. p. 645. In all these engagements, the secretariat works in close ecumenical collaboration with the Dialogue with People of Living Faiths and Ideologies of the World Council of Churches. The two bodies *or* rather offices now alternate annual meetings in Rome and Geneva. And the secretariat participates in congresses organized by the Dialogue with People of Living Faiths and Ideologies, such as

those at Cambridge (1981), Seminyak in Bali, Indonesia (1982), and Vancouver (1983).

72   Ibid. p. 645.

73   Arinze, "Interreligious Dialogue", p.18.

74   [bid. p. 18. The number of non-Christians in Europe and North America is fast increasing every year. In France, for instance, Moslems alone were six million in 1990, and it was expected that by the year 2000 they alone would constitute at least one third of the population. See *Our Sunday Visitor* [Huntington, Indiana], 13 January 1991, p. 14

75   Pope John Paul II, "The Challenge and Possibility of Peace" *Origins* 16 (November 6, 1986):370.

76   Ibid. P. 371.

77   See Origins 15(August 29, 1985): 174.

78   "*Catholic Sentinel* [Portland] September 10, 1999, p. 2.

79   Cardinal Francis Arinze, "The Urgency of Dialogue with Non-Christians", *Origins* 14 (March 14, I985):645.

80   *The Herald News* [Joliet, Illinois] January 28. 1999, p. A7.

81   ¹⁴Arinze, "The Urgency of Dialogue with N on-Christians" pp. 645-646. Ibid. p. 646

82   Ibid. p. 646.

83   Cardinal John Krol, "A Letter from the Synod", *Origins* 4(October 10. I974):252.

[84] Pope Paul VI, *Evangelii Nuntiandi* #80.

[85] *National Catholic Reporter* [Kansas City], 15 March 1991, p. 6.

[86] Elizabeth Isichei, *A History of the Igbo People* (London: The MacMillan Press, 1976), pp. 42ff.

[87] Ibid. p.68

[88] Ibid. 43-44.

[89] Ibid. 46-47.

[90] Ibid. p.47.

[91] The effects of these evils can be seen even today in some Africans and people of African origin, for instance, in the United States where the blacks have an uphill task of proving that they have human dignity; where too some blacks, because of the harsh treatment they and their ancestors have received, have either grown up to be violent or to resort to the use of drugs and alcohol for consolation.

[92] A British soldier in 1909, narrating his experience to a London audience, said that Igboland "is really a small portion of Nigeria . . . but it has been the most troublesome section of any." E. A. Steel, "Exploration in Southern Nigeria," *Journal of the Royal United Services Institution* (April 1910): 446, quoted in Elizabeth Isichei, A *History of Igbo People* p. 121.

[93] Isichei, *A History of Igbo People* pp. 119-123.

[94] Ibid. p.126-129.

[95] Ibid. p. 155.

96   See Joseph Fitzpatrick, *One Church, Many Cultures* (Kansas City. MO: Sheed and Ward. 1987), pp. 78, 84-85.

97   Vatican II, *Unitatis Redintegratio (Decree on Ecumenism),* #1.

98   Pope Paul VI, *Evangelii Nuntiandi,* #77.

99   See Arinze. "The Urgency of Dialogue with Non-Christians", p. 649.

100 Vatican II, *Nostra Aetate* #3.

101 Ibid.

102 *Origins* 14(March 1985):646.

103 *Zenit,* [international news agency] 16 November 2010, p. 1.

104 *National Catholic Register* [here-in-after NCR] 23 January 2000, p. 6.

105 NCR 27 March 2000, p.6; *The Wanderer* 24 February 2000, pp. 1 & 7.

106 *Origins* 11 (February 25, 1982): 588.

107 NCR 2-8 April 2000, p. 7.

108 Vatican II, "Declaration on Religious Liberty" *(Dignitatis Humanae)* #2.

109 *The Leader* [Owerri, Nigeria] I February 1987, p. I ; 15 February 1987. p. 1; 20 May 1 990. p. I; 3 June 1990. p. I.

110 *Catholic New York* 20 December 1990, p. 9.

[111] See "Turkish Archbishop Urges Realistic View of Islam", *The Wanderer* [St. Paul, Minnesota] 28 October 1999 pp. 1, 8.

[112] '*National Catholic Register 9* January 2000. p. I.

[113] Arinze, "The Urgency of Dialogue with Non-Christians", p. 646.

[114] Pope John Paul II. "Dialogue Between Christians and Moslems". *Origins* 15(AugList29, 1985): 174.

[115] Ibid. p.175.

[116] Ibid. pp. 175-176.

[117] Ibid. p. 176.

[118] NCR 5 March 2000, p. 13.

[119] NCR March 26-1 April 2000, p. 10.

[120] Ibid. p. 10.

[121] *Catholic Near East* May-June 2000, pp. 8-12.

[122] See Vatican.va, s.v. "Speeches of Pope John Paul II."

[123] Vatican II, *Nostra Aetate* # 2

[124] *Origins* 14(1985):647.

[125] John Paul II, "Recalling the Teaching of Mahatma Gandhi", *Origins* 15(February 20, 1986): 587.

[126] Idem, "Address to Non-Christian Leaders", ibid. p. 597.

[127] John Paul II, "The Church in a Buddhist Land", *Origins* 14(May 17, 1984):23

[128] *Origins* 14(May 14, 1985):646.

[129] Ibid. pp. 646-647.

[130] "Papal Address to Non-Christian Religions", *Origins* 4 (May 17, 1984):6.

[131] This religion has also adherents in Asia, West Indies and the Americas. In Burma, Cambodia, Laos, Thailand, and Sri Lanka, the predominant Hinayana Buddhism is deeply influenced by the ancestral cult. The same is true of Japanese Shintoism, popular Indian Hinduism, popular Chinese Taoism, and Chinese Confucianism. See Arinze, *Origins* 14 (March 14, 1985): 647; see also *World Religions: From Ancient History to the Present,* ed. Geoffrey Parrinder (New York: Fact on File Publications, 1983, p. 263.

[132] *Origins* 14(May 14, 1985):648.

[133] Ibid. p. 648.

[134] *The Catholic World Report* (January 2000), p. 22.

[135] "Day of Prayer in Assisi", *Origins* 16(November 6, 1986))370.

[136] Pope John Paul II, "The Meaning of the Assisi Day of Prayer", *Origins* 16 (January 15. 1987): 561.

[137] "Address of the Pope at the Conclusion of the Plenary Assembly of the Secretariat for Non-Christians", in *The Attitude of the Church towards the Followers of Other Religions* (Vatican City: Secretariat for Non-Christians, 1984), p. 4.

[138] *"Pilgrims of Truth, Pilgrims of Peace"*, the address of Pope Benedict XVI at the meeting for peace in Assisi on October 27, 2011.

[139] Ibid.

[140] Pope John Paul II in a radio message on 21 February 1981 to the people of Asia quoted in *The Christian Faith,* ed. J. Neuner and J. Dupuis (New York: Alba House, 1982). p. 300.

[141] Karl Rahner, *Foundations of Christian Faith* (New York: Crossroads Publishing Company, 1978), p. 251.

[142] *The New Dictionary of Theology* (1987) s. v. "The Reign of God", by Donald Senior.

[143] Saul's rejection and fall, for instance, were due to the fact that he failed to observe this rule. See 1 Samuel 15: 10-23, 13:13-14.

[144] 1 Sam 8: 1-8.

[145] 2 Kings 17 and 24; see also Isaiah 44: 24, 26-45: 6; Zephaniah 3:14-16.

[146] Antiochus Epiphanes is considered one of the most heartless of Israel's oppressors. See Daniel 9:27; I Maccabees 1:54.

[147] This hope is expressed in apocalyptic writings, for instance, Daniel 2:44; 7:14. Since the Israelites had the hope that God himself would establish his reign or kingdom, to claim to proclaim the coming of this kingdom, as Jesus would do later, implied ushering it in. It was therefore a claim of a prerogative of God.

[148] Isaiah 26:19; 29:18f; 61:1; and especially 35:5ff.

149 Walter Kasper, *Jesus the Christ* (New York: Paulist Press, 1976), p. 75.

150 Karl Rahner, *Foundations of Christian Faith* p. 254; James D.G. Dunn, *Christology in the Making* (Philadelphia: Westminster Press, 1980), p. 253f.

151 Kasper op. cit. p.102.

152 Karl Rahner, *Foundations of Christian Faith* p. 253; Walter Kasper, *Jesus the Christ* p. 102

153 Edward Schillebeeckx, *Jesus* (New York: Seabury Press, 1979), p. 189; also Kasper, op. cit. p. 91.

154 Kasper, op. cit. pp. 102ff; Schillebeeckx, op. cit. pp. 219ff.

155 Kasper, op. cit. p. 101; see also Schillebeeckx, op. cit. pp 200; Richard Viladesau, *Answering For Faith* (New York: Paulist Press, 1987), p. 203.

156 Rahner, *Foundation of Christian Faith p.* 254; Viladesau, op. cit. p. 204; c.f. also Mk. 10;45; 14;24; 8:31-33 and parallels.

157 Rahner, *Foundations of Christian Faith p.* 264.

158 C.f. Mk.8:31; 9:31; 10: 34, and par. See Donald Senior, *The Passion of Jesus in the Gospel of Mark (Wilmington,* Delaware: Michael Glazier, 1984) pp.l35ff.

159 Rahner, *Foundations of Christian Faith,* p. 266.

160 Rahner, ibid. 266. The fact that resurrection is not a mere return to mortal life can be ascertained in Paul who points out that a

resurrected body is immortal and quite different from the earthly body. See 1 Cor. 15:35-44.

161 Rahner, *Foundations of Christian Faith* p. 267.

162 Rahner, ibid. pp. 268-272.

163 Dennis and Matthew Linn with Sheila Fabricant, *Healing the Greatest Hurt* (New York: Paulist Press, 1985), pp 4 1f.

164 See *The Lives of the Saints* ed. Hugo Hoever (New York: Catholic Book Publishing Co., 1989). p.337. Other examples abound in daily life, such as the cases of anonymous donors to charity and those who, without any compulsion or hope for material gain, risk their lives to take care of patients of dangerous contagious or infectious diseases.

165 Rahner, *Foundations of Christian Faith* p. 273. It may be pointed out here that for the Igbo people of Nigeria and Africans in general, whether they are Christians or not, life after physical death is quite real. This offers them an important help in understanding or rather believing the resurrection of Jesus.

166 Karl Rahner, *Foundations of Christian Faith,* p.274.

167 See Deuteronomy 21:23; Galatians 3:13; 1 Cor. 1:23.

168 The Easter experience which was quite unique was made available only to that precise phase of the history of salvation, the apostolic phase, and to no other. While a person is free to refuse to believe the apostolic witnesses, this person cannot do so by pretending that he understands their experience better than they did. And to reject the message of the resurrection of Jesus in such a way that this rejection also denies the transcendental hope in resurrection is to deny one's very existence. See Karl Rahner, *Foundations of Christian Faith* pp.

274ff; Peter C. Phan, *Eternity in Time* (Cranbury, N.J: Associated University Presses, 1988), p. 162

169   Richard Viladesau, *Answering For Faith p.* 210.

170   Karl Rahner. *Foundations* pp. 276-278; Richard Viladesau, *Answering For Faith* pp. 21 0 ff; also *The New Dictionary of Theology* (1987) s.v. "The Resurrection of Christ" by Gerald O' Collins. See also Perkins Pheme. *Resurrection: New Testament Witness and Contemporary Reflection* (Garden City, New York: Doubleday & Co. Inc., 1984) p. 34.

171   Karl Rahner, *Foundations,* p. 280.

172   John P. Schanz, *Introduction To The Sacraments* (New York: Pueblo Publishing Company, 1983), p. 33.

173   Kasper, op. cit. p. 103.

174   John 14: 2-3.

175   Vatican II: *Gaudium et Spes* #22; Pope John Paul II, *Redemptor Hominis* (Washington D. C.: Office of Publishing Services, United States Catholic Conference, 1979), #13 and #14. In the light of this new knowledge gained about the meaning of man Karl Rahner rightly maintains that Christology is the beginning and end of anthropology. Karl Rahner, *Foundations* pp. 224-225.

176   Rahner, *Foundations,* p. 284.

177   DS1639.

178   Avery Dulles, *Models of the Church* (Garden City, New York: Doubleday & Company. Inc., 1974). p.63.

[179] Karl Rahner. "The Theology of the Symbol", *Theological Investigations* 20 vols. (Baltimore: Helicon Press, and London: Darton, Longman & Todd. 1961-1981:4 (1966)221-252; see also A very Dulles. *Models of Revelation* (Garden City, New York: Image Books, 1985), p. 157.

[180] Michael Schmaus. *DOGMAM 4: The Church: Its Origin and Structure* (Kansas City and London: Sheed and Ward. 1972). p. 19;

[181] Vatican II, *Sacrosanctum Concilium* or *Constitution on Sacred Liturgy* (here-in-after CSL) #7.

[182] Karl Rahner. "The Episcope and the Primacy", *Inquiries* (New York: Herder and Herder. 1964), p. 317; also Avery Dulles, *Models of the Church* (New York: Image Books, 1987). pp.63ff. The conversion of Saul the Pharisee and persecutor of the Church to the missionary Apostle Paul is a good pointer to the fact that the Church is the historical continuation of Christ. See Acts 9; I ff: 22: 3-16; *The New Jerome Biblical Commentary;* (.1990). #77:20-23.

[183] Vatican II, *Constitution on the Church* (here-in-after *Lumen Gentium* or Simply *LG*) #1.

[184] John L. McKenzie, *Dictionary of the Bible,* s.v. covenant.

[185] A symbolic action is an action performed to stand for an event that is imminent and irrevocable. It was used by the prophets, especially Ezekiel, in very important messages. For instance, in Ezk. 12:1-18, the prophet performed an action which was symbolic of the imminent and irrevocable exile that the Israelites were about to go to. Other examples are Ezk. 4:1-5:1 7; Is. 20: lff; Jer. 13:1-11; 16: I ff; 19:1-13; Ezk.24.15ff. Jesus' Last Supper was a symbolic action that stands for his imminent and irrevocable death. After his death and resurrection, the celebration or rather re-enactment of

that Supper becomes the sacrament of his death and resurrection and hence a celebration which promotes the growth of the Church and the welfare of the world.

[186] This is why during the celebration of the Jewish Passover the youngest member of the family asks the father of the family for the meaning of the celebration. And the father or elder of the family tells the story of the salvation or rescue of Israel from Egypt by God's intervening love: see Ex. 12:26-27.

[187] John L. Mckenzie, *Dictionary of the Bible,* s.v. "Eucharist."

[188] Michael Schmaus op. cit. p. 22.

[189] Ibid. p. 24.

[190] Ibid. p. 33.

[191] Ibid. p. 36.

[192] Raymond *E.* Brown, *An Introduction to the New Testament* (New York: Doubleday 1997*),* p. 221; *The Collegeville Bible Commentary,* ed. Dianne Bergant & Robert J. Harris (Collegeville, Minnesota: Liturgical Press 1989), p. 885.

[193] Schmaus op. cit. p.37.

[194] Ibid. p. 38.

[195] See ibid. 41-42.

[196] Cf. Lumen Gentium #20: Catechism of the Catholic Church #861.

[197] Congregation for The Doctrine of the Faith, *Declaration "Dominic Jesus"* [August 6, 2000] #16.

[198] Ibid. #16 &17.

[199] Lumen Gentium #1.

[200] Saint Cyprian developed this maxim while dealing with the problem of schism. He argues that as there was no escape for anyone outside the ark of Noah so also there is no escape or salvation for anyone outside the Church. Cf. Cyprian. "The Unity of the Catholic Church" 6. in *The Lapsed and the Unity of the Catholic Church* (Westminster, Maryland: The Newman Press. 1957). p.49.

[201] Paul Knitter, *No Other Name?* (Mary knoll, New York: Orbis Books. 1985). pp. 75-76.

[202] The basic teaching of the conservative Evangelicals today is essentially the same as Barth's position. See James Davison Hunter, *Evangelism* (Chicago: The University of Chicago Press. 1987). pp. 20ff, 34ff

[203] Barth's teaching is taken from his *Church Dogmatics 4* vols. (Edinburgh: T & Clark. 1956-1970). vol. I, second-half [1/2] vol. : *The Doctrine of the Word of God*

[204] Barth, *The Doctrine of the Word of God* p. 280

[205] Ibid. p. 301.

[206] Ibid. pp. 301-302.

[207] Ibid. pp. 306-308.

[208] Ibid. pp. 307ff.

[209] Ibid. pp.299-300.

210 Ibid. pp.352ff. Here Barth is employing Martin Luther's theology of justification, according to which the sinner is justified not by his own merit or good work, but by the imputation of the righteousness of Christ. See Martin Luther, *Lectures on Romans,* trans. Hilton C. Oswald (St. Louis: Concordia Publishing House, 1972), pp. 259-260; see also "The Freedom of a Christian" in the *Selected Writings of Martin Luther,* ed. Theodoret G. Tapper (Philadelphia: Fortress Press, 1967), p. 28.

211 Barth, op. cit. pp. 325-326

212 Ibid. p. 338.

213 Ibid. p. 356; see also Paul Knitter, *No Other Name?* p. 85.

214 Barth, op. cit. p. 347.

215 Ibid. p. 297.

216 John Hick is the best known advocate of this position. See Paul Knitter, op. cit. p.147.

217 John Hick, *God Has Many Names* (Philadelphia: The Westminster Press, 1982), pp.13-20

218 Ibid. p. 18.

219 Ibid. pp.45-56.

220 Ibid. p. 36f; see also pp. 69ff.

221 Ibid. p.58

222 Ibid. p. 74; also "Jesus and the World Religions" in *The Myth of God Incarnate,* ed. John Hick (Philadelphia: The Westminster Press, 1977), p. 178.

223 "Jesus and the World Religions", p. 167; also *God Has Many Names* p. 73f, and "The Non-Absoluteness of Christianity" *in The Myth of Christian Uniqueness,* ed. John Hick and Paul F. Knitter (Maryknoll, New York: Orbis Books, 1987), p. 31.

224 "Jesus and the World Religions", p. 168.

225 Ibid. p. 169-170.

226 Ibid. pp. 170-171.

227 Hick, *God Has Many Names,* p.75.

228 Vatican II, *Lumen Gentium* #8.

229 Vatican II, *Lumen Gentium* #14. The Church rejects, however, the view of Father Leonard Feeney and his group, who held that there was no salvation for anyone outside the Roman Catholic Church; that is, the view that only Roman Catholics can be saved. See Francis A. Sullivan, *Salvation Outside the Church?* (New York/ Mahwah, N.J.: Paulist Press, 1992), pp. 135ff.

230 Vatican II, *Lumen Gentium* #14.

231 Vatican II, *Unitas Redintegratio (Decree on Ecumenism) #3; Lumen Gentium* #15

232 Vatican II, *Unitas Redintegratio* #13-18; the *Catechism of the Catholic Church* # 838.

233 Vatican II, *Lumen Gentium,* #16.

[234] Karl Rahner, "Concerning the Relationship between Nature and Grace" [here-in-after, "Relationship", *Theological Investigations* 1 (1961)310-313.

[235] Ibid. pp. 313-315.

[236] Karl Rahner, "Anonymous Christians", *Theological Investigations*[6] *(*1969)393; also idem, "On the Theology of the Incarnation", *Theological Investigations 4 (1966)* 110; idem *Foundations of Christian Faith pp.* 224-225.

[237] Vatican II, *Gaudium et Spes (The Church in the Modern World)* #22; see also Pope John Paul II, Redemptor Hominis #13 & #14.

[238] Rahner, "History of the World and Salvation History", *Theological Investigations,* 5(1966) 103-104; idem, "Anonymous Christians" pp. 393-394.

[239] Vatican II, *Lumen Gentium* #16.

[240] John 14:6.

[241] Pontifical Council for Inter-religious Dialogue and The Congregation for the Evangelization of Peoples, "Dialogue and Proclamation" #29 in *Origins* 21 (July 4, 1991)127.

[242] *Catechism of the Catholic Church* #1260.

[243] DS 1524; see *Catechism* #1258.

[244] Vatican II, *Gaudium et Spes* #22.

[245] "Dialogue and Proclamation" #68; see also *Gaudium et Spes #22.*

[246] Most biblical scholars have no doubt that Jesus did commission his followers to preach the good news to all parts of 'the world. See *The New Jerome Biblical Commentary,* ed. Raymond Brown et al. (Eaglewood Cliffs. New Jersey: Prentice Hall, 1990), #42:168; see also *The Collegeville Bible Commentary,* ed. Dianne Bergant and Robert Karris (Collegeville, Minnesota: The Liturgical Press, 1989). p. 902.

[247] Vatican II *Ad Gentes* #7. The council makes similar statements in most parts of this document and also in several other documents.

[248] Article 25 of the bishops' working paper, "Evangelization in the Modem World", *Origins* 4(August 29, 1974) 150.

[249] Pope Paul VI, *Evangelii Nuntiandi #5.*

[250] Ibid. #53.

[251] Pope John Paul II. *Redemptoris Missio* #7. The pastoral letter was dated December 7. 1990, the 25th anniversary of the Second Vatican Council's decree on the Church's missionary activity, *Ad Gentes,* but released at the Vatican on January 22, 1991. The text was in *Catholic New York* of February 7, 1991.

[252] Pope John Paul IL *Redemptoris Missio* #16.

[253] Pope Paul VI, *Evangelii Nuntiandi* #17.

[254] Ibid. #18

[255] Ibid. #19.

[256] Ibid. #20 & #22.

257 Vatican II, *Missionary Activity or Ad Gentes (here-in-after Ad Gentes or Simply AG)* #11.

258 Ibid. #12

259 Vatican II, *The Church in the Modern World* or *Gaudium et Spes (here-in-after Gaudium et Spes)* #43.

260 Pope Paul VI, *Evangelii Nuntiandi #21 & #41.*

261 Ibid. #15. See also #16 & #10.

262 Pope John Paul II, *Redemptoris Missio* #42.

263 Ibid. #43.

264 Ibid. #44.

265 Pope Paul VI, *Evangelii Nuntiandi*

266 Pope John Paul II, *Redemptoris Missio* #45.

267 Pope Paul VI, *Evangelii Nuntiandi* #26: cf. also Bede McGregor. "Commentary on *Evangelii Nuntiandi*" in *Evangelization Today,* ed. Austin Flannery (Northport. New York: Costello Publishing Company, 1977), pp. 69-75.

268 Evangelii Nuntiandi #27; see also John Paul II, *Redemptoris Hominis* #44

269 *Evangelii Nuntiandi* #28.

270 Ibid. #29.

271 Ibid. #31.

272 Pope John Paul II, *Redemptoris Missio* #60; see also the 3rd General Conference of Latin American Bishops, *Puebla: La Evangelizacion en el Presente y en el Futuro de America Latina* (Claveria, Mexico: Libreria, Parroquial, 1984), #1142; *Evangelii Nuntiandi #38.*

273 E*vangelii Nuntiandi.* #32-34; quotation from #33; also Pope John Paul II, *Redemptoris Missio* #17.

274 "¹Pope John Paul II, *Redemptoris Missio* #59; *Evangelii Nuntiandi* #35-#37.

275 Vatican II, *Inter Mirifica (Decree on the Means of Social Communication)* #1

276 Ibid. #13.

277 Ibid. #17.

278 Pontifical Council for the Instruments of Social Communication, "Communi et Progresso", 29 January 1971, #126; *Evangelii Nuntiandi* #45.

279 *Evangelii Nuntiandi* #46.

280 Redemptoris Missio #63—#71.

281 Justin Ukpong. "Emergence of African Theologies", *Theological Studies 45(1984):514-515.*

282 Extraordinary Synod of Bishops of 1985, "The Final Report" in *Origins* 15 (December 19, 1985)450; also *Redemptoris Missio* #52.

283 Joseph Fitzpatrick, *One Church, Many Cultures* (Kansas City, MO: Sheed & Ward. 1987), P. 64.

[284] Ibid. pp. 67-72.

[285] Ibid. pp. 78, 84-85.

[286] Pope John Paul II, "Father Matteo Ricci: Bridge to China", *The Pope Speaks* 28:2(1983): 100, 102.

[287] Aylward Shorter, *Theology of Mission* (Notre Dame. Indiana: Fides Publishers, 1972), pp. 55-56.

[288] Avery Dulles, *Models of the Church,* p.68.

[289] Vatican II, *Ad Gentes* #22.

[290] Idem, *Gaudium et Spes* #58: see also *The New Dictionary of Theology* (1987), s.v. "Inculturation" by Eugene Hillman.

[291] *Evangelii Nuntiandi* #3.

[292] Ibid. #20.

[293] Pope John Paul II, "Carry the Authentic Gospel to the African Culture", *The Pope Speaks* 25:4(1980)299: see also Pope John Paul II, *Catechesi Tradendae* (Boston. Daughters of St. Paul. 1979), #53.

[294] Pope John Paul II. "To the Bishops of Nigeria," *Origins* 11: 37 (February 25, 1982): 586.

[295] Idem, *Redemptoris Missio* #52 & #53.

[296] Evangelization of culture does not necessarily mean that every individual within the culture has been converted. What it means is that the environment has been adequately challenged by the gospel

message. This, all things being equal, can make the conversion of individuals easier. See Aylward Shorter, *Theology of Mission* #55.

297   Vatican II, *Dignitatis Humanae* # 1

298   Ibid. #3; also #9, # 10.

299   Ibid. #12 & #14

300   See Cardinal Francis Arinze, "Christian—Muslim Relations in the 21st Century", *The Leader* [Owerri] 12 July 1998, p. 8.

301   Pope John Paul II, *Tertio Millennio Adveniente* Apostolic Letter to the Bishops, Clergy, and Lay Faithful on Preparation for the Jubilee of the Year *2000, #33.*

302   See *National Catholic Register 26* March-1 April 2000, p. 4.

303   Ibid.

304   *Time* [magazine] 3 April 2000   p.34.

305   AII that the Church asks is that Moslems reciprocate its goodwill by allowing Christians in Moslem countries freedom of worship. See Cardinal Francis Arinze, "Christian-Muslim Relations in the 21st Century", *The Leader* [Owerri] *12   July 1998, p. 8.*

306   Ibid.

307   Fernando Capala, "A Dialogue of Life and Faith," *Columbian Mission* [Nebraska], October 1990, pp. 3-5.

308   Ibid. pp. 10, 13, & 18..

[309] *Maryknoll* (Maryknoll, New York; Maryknoll Fathers and Brothers, December *1999), pp. 14-21.*

[310] Ibid. p. 26.

[311] This, surely, does not mean that Christians should not help needy non-Christians. But help should not be given as a condition for non-Christians to accept the good news. See Vatican II, *Dignitatis Humanae (Declaration on Religious Freedom)* #12.

[312] The following statement of Hans Kung tends to give this impression: "Christianity . . . should perform its service among the world religions in a dialectical unity of recognition and rejection, as a critical catalyst and crystallization point of their religious, moral, meditative, ascetic, aesthetic values . . . But this would not mean that it has to be directed to winning the greatest possible number of converts. The real aim would be to enter into genuine dialogue with the religions as a whole." Hans Kung, *On Being a Christian* (New York: Doubleday & Company, 1976), p. 112. See also Walter Kasper, "Absoluteness of Christianity," *Sacramentum Mundi,* vol. 1, ed. Karl Rahner (New York: Herder and Herder, 1968), p. 312.

[313] Pope Paul VI, *Evangelii Nuntiandi* #23; see also Pope John Paul II, *Redemptoris Missio* #46.

[314] *Evangelii Nuntiandi* #23, 24.

[315] Vatican II, *Ad Gentes* #9.

[316] Pontifical Council for Inter-religious Dialogue and the Congregation for the Evangelization of Peoples, "Dialogue and Proclamation" #35, *Origins 21* (July 4. 1991) p. 128; cf. also *Lumen Gentium* #8.

[317] *The Wanderer (St.* Paul, Minnesota) 10 February 2000, pp. I & 7; see also *National Catholic Register* 6 February 2000, p. 5.

318 Declaration *"Dominus Jesus"* #20-22. [The document was dated August 6 but was published on September 5, 2000.]

319 Pope John Paul II, *Tertio Millenio Advente* #6.

320 Ibid.

321 Pope Paul VI, *Evangelii Nuntiandi* #80.

322 'The Paulist National Catholic Evangelization Association, *National Association of Catholic Business and Professional Men and Women* (Washington D.C.; The Paulist National Catholic Evangelization Association, 1990), p. 2.

323 See *National Catholic Register* 19 December 1999. p. 8.

324 "A 'B' Grade Started Boy's Satan Worship," *New York Newsday 12 January 1988, p. 2.*

325 Russell Chandler, *Understanding the New Age* (Dallas: World Publishing, 1988), pp. 255ff.

326 Ibid. p. 17.

327 Ibid. pp. 20 & 253.

328 "Satan's Songs," *New York Post* 5 March 1990, p. 1.

329 "Pilgrims of Truth, Pilgrims of Peace", address of Pope Benedict XVI at the meeting of leaders of world religions at Assisi on October 27, 2011.

330 See "The Missionary's Task-Difficulties and Possibilities", *Origins* 14 (April 4, 1985):692.

[331] See Walter Martin, *The Kingdom of the Cults* (Minneapolis, Minnesota: Bethany House Publishers, 1977), pp. 7 and passim.

[332] Vatican Report on Sects, Cults and New Religious Movements, *Origins* 16 (May 22, 1986):3.

[333] James LeBar, *Cults, Sects and the New Age (Huntington,* Indiana: Our Sunday Visitor Publishing Division, 1989), p, 15.

[334] Ibid. pp. 13-14.

[335] Ibid. p. 17.

[336] Walter Martin, op. cit. pp. 30, 40.

[337] Ibid. p.106.

[338] Leonard & Marjorie Chretien, *Witnesses of Jehovah* (Eugene, Oregon: Harvest House Publishers. 1988), p. 40"

[339] Ibid. pp. 42-43.

[340] Ibid. p. 44.

[341] Ibid. pp. 44-46.

[342] Ibid. pp. 46, 50.

[343] Ibid. p 13.

[344] Ibid. p. 14.

[345] Ibid. pp. 59 & 61.

[346] "Ugandan Massacre Death Toll Nears 600." *The Bulletin* [Bend Oregon] 28 March 2000, p. A7.

[347] See Walter Martin, *The Kingdom of the Cults* p. 336. The Witnesses, who always misinterpret Scripture, also cite John 14:28 as their basis for placing Jesus lower than God the Father. But they do not read also John 10:30 and John 14:9f.

[348] Leonard & Marjorie Chretien, *Witnesses of Jehovah* p. 61.

[349] Walter Martin, op. cit. pp. 24-25.

[350] Ibid. pp. 27-31.

[351] Ibid. pp. 147-149.

[352] Ihid, p. 326.

[353] Ibid. p. 31.

[354] Stanley Krippner & Albert Villoldo, *The Realms of Healing,* new rev, ed. (Millbrae, California: Celestial Arts, 1976). p. 111.

[355] Ibid. p. 116.

[356] Francis MacNutt, *The Power to Heal* (Notre Dame. Indiana: Ave Maria Press, 1977), p. 75

[357] James J. LeBar, *Cults, Sects, and the New Age* (Huntington, Indiana: Our Sunday Visitor Publishing Division, 1989), pp.27-28.

[358] Donna Steichen, *The Ungodly Rage* (San Francisco—Ignatius Press. 1991), p. 41.

359 Many young people (former Catholics) in the United States, when asked why they left the Church complained that the Mass or liturgy was dead and did not appeal to them.

360 Francis MacNutt, *Healing* (Notre Dame, Indiana: Ave Maria Press, 1974) pp. 38ff.

361 See, for instance, Ephesians 6: 10-18.

362 See Gabriel Amorth, *The Exorcist Tell His Story* (San Francisco: Ignatius Press, 1999), pp. 37f

363 General Audience of Pope Paul VI on November 15, 1972, reported in the L'Osservatare Romano, Nov. 23 1972; see also "The Devil's Place", *Origins* 2 (December 7, 1972):391-392.

364 This document was dated June 26, 1975. The text can be found in *Vatican Council II: More Post Conciliar Documents,* ed. Austin Flannery (North- port,

365 Ralph M. McInerny, *What Went Wrong with Vatican II?* (Manchester, New Hampshire: Sophia Institute Press, 1998), pp. 31-34.

366 Vatican II, *Lumen Gentium* #22.

367 Randy England, *The Unicorn in the Sanctuary: The Impact of the New Age on the Catholic Church* (Manssas, Va.: Trinity Communications, 1990), p. 130.

368 Ibid. p. 130.

369 Donna Steichen, *Ungodly Rage: The Hidden Face of Catholic Feminism* (San Francisco: Ignatius Press, 1991), pp. 40-41.

370 Kieran C. Okoro, *Catechesis in the Catechumnate and Other Periods of the R.C.I.A.: A Handbook for Religious and Moral Instructions, 2ⁿᵈ ed.* (Owerri: Peace-wise Systems, 2005), p. 51.

371 See, for instance, *Ecclesia in Africa—Post Synodal Apostolic Exhortation Of Pope John Paul II to the Bishops and Christians of Africa* [1995] #73-85.

372 Ibid. #86-98.